W9-BJH-301

W9-BJH-301

THE COLOURGUIDE TO
VEGETABLE GROWING

The Colour Guide To
VEGETABLE GROWING

Tom Wellsted

TREASURE PRESS

Contents

First published in Great Britain in 1980 by
Octopus Books Limited under the title
Home-grown Vegetables
This edition published in 1986 by
Treasure Press
59 Grosvenor Street London W1
© 1980 Hennerwood Publications Limited
Reprinted 1986
ISBN 1 85051 101 2
Printed in Hong Kong

Growing your own

There are many good reasons why, even in the relatively restricted space available in typical suburban gardens, more and more people are growing their own vegetables. On the face of it the price of vegetables in the shops and markets is an obvious reason, although the economies possible in raising your own are often more apparent than real – especially if you take the view that time equals money. For instance, if you are not fussy about the types of peas you eat, it may not be worth the effort to grow them when reasonably priced frozen peas are available all the year round. The smaller the space available in your vegetable garden, the greater the weight you should give to economic considerations of this kind; and this applies especially to crops, such as potatoes, that take up a good deal of space. On the other hand, it may well make economic sense to grow an especially early variety of a vegetable, which will be ready for the table when its price in the shops is still relatively high.

Most vegetable gardeners, however, grow their own for other, and better, reasons than economic ones: quality, freshness, and range of choice. Among certain commercially grown vegetables consideration is given to such things as uniformity of size and shape and the ability to travel well. These properties are largely irrelevant to the value of such vegetables in the kitchen and may, indeed, have been achieved at some cost in flavour. The superiority, in terms of crispness, aroma, or flavour, of freshly picked lettuce and tomatoes over most shop-bought ones is too well known to need enlarging upon here. The same applies to most other home-grown vegetables; young runner beans, for instance, are delicious when cooked whole, and French beans are much richer in flavour if cooked when absolutely fresh. Nowhere, however, is freshness more important than in the case of herbs, which in many shop-bought examples have inevitably lost some of their scent and flavour-giving properties.

When it comes to choice, the advantages of home-grown vegetables are threefold. First, of course, is the fact that your cropping programmes can include some species of vegetables that are seldom, if ever, available at your local greengrocer. Second, your choice is enormously expanded, in the case of many vegetables, by the number of varieties available. For instance, although potatoes take up a lot of space, you may have a particular liking for a certain variety, such as 'Pink Fir Apple', that you are unlikely to find in the shops. The third advantage, already referred to, is that you can raise certain crops at times of the year when they are expensive to buy or are unavailable.

Finally, and perhaps decisively for many gardeners, is the pleasure and satisfaction of raising and eating vegetables one has grown oneself. The rewards are beyond any mundane questions of cost-effectiveness.

Planning the Plot

The quantity and variety of vegetables you can grow will of course depend largely on the size of your plot. The smaller the plot, the more selective you will have to be in your choice of crops. But many factors may influence your choice. You may, for instance, decide to concentrate solely on a few favourite vegetables or cultivars; or you may grow those that are usually expensive to buy; or you may limit yourself to growing crops for harvesting at times when they are unlikely to be available at the greengrocer's.

When planning your cropping programmes bear in mind that plantings need not be confined solely to the vegetable plot. Attractive herbs such as bay and rosemary and vegetables such as artichokes and ruby chard can just as easily be grown in ornamental beds and borders to relieve the pressure on space elsewhere. You may also have areas of unused space near a back door or against a house or garden wall which receives a fair amount of sun. These areas are ideal for certain crops grown in containers of various sizes. All the herbs listed will thrive in pots, or they may be raised in window boxes. Tomatoes will almost certainly do better in a grow bag against a wall than if they are planted in garden soil. Radishes, carrots, marrows, and lettuces should all do well in tubs filled with composts suitable for their specific needs.

Yields

The table below shows typical yields for some popular vegetables; it does not include crops such as cabbage and cauliflower, of which the yields obviously depend on the number of plants allowed to grow. The weights or quantities refer to a single row 1·5 m (5 ft) long, with plants spaced according to the notes on each crop in Chapter 4. Bear in mind that yields are influenced by many factors, including siting of garden, soil type, weather, time of harvesting (early potatoes, for instance, normally have a smaller yield than the main crop), cultivar selected, and attack by pests and diseases.

Asparagus	2·75 kg (6 lb)
Beans, broad	5·5 kg (12 lb)
Beans, French	3·5 kg (7¾ lb)
Beans, runner	5·5 kg (12 lb)
Beetroot	2·5 kg (5½ lb)
Brussels sprouts	1·5 kg (3¼ lb)
Carrots	2 kg (4½ lb)
Celeriac	2·5 kg (5½ lb)
Courgettes	1 kg (2¼ lb)
Cucumbers, outdoor	8–10 fruits; weight varies with type
Leaf beet	3·5 kg (7¾ lb)
Leeks	2 kg (4½ lb)
Marrows and squashes	9–15 kg (20–33 lb)
Peas	1 kg (2¼ lb)
Potatoes	3·5 kg (7¾ lb)
Shallots	About 10 bulbs per plant
Spinach	1·75 kg (4 lb)
Swedes	2·25 kg (5 lb)
Tomatoes	1·75–2·75 kg (4–6 lb) per plant
Turnips	1·25 kg (2¾ lb)

Space-saving

The total usable yield of the kitchen garden can be maximised by careful planning. Even if you have plenty of space there is little point in making one large, annual sowing of, say, carrots or beetroot because a sizeable proportion of your harvest is likely to become old and flavourless before you have a chance to eat it. A better policy is to make smaller sowings at intervals during the season; these will enable you to use a crop as soon as it is harvested. Successional crops, as these are called, allow you to use your plot more flexibly. For instance,

when broad beans, early peas, or early potatoes have been harvested, the vacant rows can be sown with lettuce, radish, spring onions, early carrots, or turnips (either for greens or roots).

Another yield-improving method is intercropping – growing plants in the spaces between rows of other crops. Intercropping needs to be planned with care because the plants will absorb water and soil nutrients that may be needed by the crops in the rows on either side. For this reason intercrops should be sown at such a time that they will mature either earlier or later than the main crops. Ideally, intercrops should be quick-maturing plants that do not take up much space. A variety of intercropping programmes is possible. For example, if you are growing brassicas (cabbages, etc) in a nursery plot for transplanting in summer, you can sow intercrops such as early beetroot, carrots, and lettuces before

Intercropping is one method of making maximum use of a given area of soil. Here calabrese broccoli and lettuce are being grown between rows of onions.

the brassicas are moved to the main plot. These crops will then be ready for harvesting before the brassicas have a chance to smother them with their leaves. Other plants, such as radishes, which take up little space can be intercropped with a wide variety of main crops.

The soil

You will get good, tasty crops only if you grow your vegetables in healthy soil. The growing medium (topsoil) consists mainly of eroded particles of rock, decomposed organic matter (humus), various mineral salts, water, and air. The consistency of a soil depends on the proportions of each of these components. At one extreme is clay, with very small rock particles; at the other is sand or gravel, with coarse particles. Clay soils are often cold and heavy: when dry they are hard, making it difficult for plant roots to spread; in wet weather they may become waterlogged and kill plants owing to the absence of air. Sandy or gravelly soils, with their more open structure, may allow water and soil nutrients to drain away, so that plants may sicken or die from lack of moisture or food. Chalky or limy soils are usually rather shallow and lacking in humus, and tend to become sticky in winter.

You cannot change the basic character of the soil in your kitchen garden but you can do much to improve it. The poor draining qualities of heavy clay soils can be alleviated by mixing in sand – preferably what is known as sharp sand, in which the particles have jagged edges that make it more difficult for water droplets to cling to them. Clays also benefit greatly by the addition of organic materials, such as garden compost or manure, and of peat, which has little or no food value but helps to open up the soil structure. Light, sandy soils and chalky soils need to be improved with bulky organic materials; farmyard manure is ideal for this, but as it is not easily obtainable you will probably have to make do with garden compost.

Soils are also classified according to whether they are acid, alkaline, or neutral. You can determine the status of your kitchen-garden soil with one of the inexpensive soil-testing kits available from garden centres. It is worth doing this because some vegetables are intolerant of certain soils; brassicas, for instance, will not thrive in acid soils. A neutral or slightly alkaline soil is satisfactory for most purposes. Acid soils can be made alkaline by the addition of hydrated lime; this will also improve the structure of acid clay soils.

Fertilisers

In addition to sunlight, water, and air plants need about a dozen nutrient elements for healthy growth. The humus in good soil contains most or all of these; so, too, do garden compost and farmyard manure. But you will almost certainly need to add proprietary fertilisers to your soil unless you have a regular source of good, bulky farmyard manure or make your own garden compost.

The three most important elements are nitrogen, phosphorus, and potassium, whose scientific abbreviations are N, P, and K respectively; three other major elements are calcium (C), magnesium (Mg), and sulphur (S). Plants also need minute quantities of boron (B), copper (Cu), iron (Fe), manganese (Mn), molybdenum (Mo), and zinc (Zn), which are known collectively as trace elements. Proprietary brands of general fertilisers are based on N, P, and K in varying proportions and many include some of the other elements as well. You can also buy fertilisers based on any one of the first six elements mentioned above. The notes on specific crops in Chapter 4 indicate any particular needs.

Some gardeners prefer to use natural fertilisers (garden compost, manure, and powdered organic materials such as bone meal, hoof-and-horn meal, and dried blood) rather than proprietary ones. In terms purely of food value, neither type is better than the other; but they differ in the speed at which the elements are taken up by plants. The proprietary fertilisers act quicker – and this is especially true of the foliar feeds, which are sprayed onto the plant leaves. On the other hand, the organic fertilisers, because they are slower acting, have a beneficial effect over a longer period. They also retain moisture and warmth – the latter an important advantage if you are growing crops such as marrows.

Mulches

Mulching involves placing a layer of material over the soil to prevent evaporation of moisture, to discourage weeds, and in general to help keep the soil in good condition. A

A well-stocked vegetable garden, with paved pathways between the plots.

variety of mulching materials can be used, from organic substances to plastic sheeting. Compost, manure, leaf mould, and other organic mulches have the additional advantage in that water will pass through them, collecting plant-feeding matter on the way. Mulches are usually applied in spring; always water the soil before applying an impervious mulch such as plastic. Mulching requirements for specific plants are given in Chapter 4.

Digging

Digging aerates and improves the structures of all but the lightest soils; it is essential if the soil has not been used for crop growing for several years or if a hard pan has developed beneath the topsoil. A hard pan forms at a depth of about 300 mm (1 ft). As it is more or less impervious to water it prevents the topsoil from draining properly, and so it must be broken up with a spade or fork before you begin cultivation.

Ideally you should dig to about double the spade depth, since many common vegetables are deep-rooters. If you are cultivating the soil for the

Enriching soil with manure is best done in the autumn. Make sure that the soil and manure (or compost) are well mixed.

first time, dig in as much well-rotted organic material as possible; manure, compost, and leaf mould are all suitable, and if your soil is poor they may need to be dug in every year. Make sure that the material is well worked in, so that the soil has the same colour and consistency to a depth of about 450 mm (18 in). If possible, do the annual dig in autumn or early winter. This will allow the soil and extra organic material to become thoroughly integrated before your spring plantings; early digging is especially important if you are adding lime to the soil.

Rotation

One of the most important ways to maintain the productivity of the kitchen garden is by rotational cropping. This involves growing particular vegetables, or closely related ones, in different plots in the garden each year. There are two main reasons for this. First, a particular group of vegetables has different soil and food needs from other groups, so that if you grow the same group on the same plot year after year the soil will eventually lose its fertility. The second reason is that soil pests and diseases that affect that particular group will be encouraged to in-

ABOVE RIGHT When preparing the soil, dig as deep as possible. Take out a trench (left), piling earth at the side. Break up underlying soil with a fork (centre) and work in manure. Move soil from next trench (right) into first.

BELOW RIGHT Three-year rotation: crops and soil treatment. Left-hand column (first year) from top to bottom: peas, beans, salad crops, and onions (add manure, compost, or peat); cabbage family (add fertiliser and lime); potatoes and root vegetables (add fertiliser only). Middle column represents second year, right-hand column third year.

crease if the group is always grown in the same plot. Rotation can also help you to economise on organic materials. You will, for instance, have to add compost or manure to the plot on which you are to grow beans or marrows; but the following year the same plot can be planted with other crops that do not need the addition of organic materials. Again, rotation helps you to take advantage of the fact that the roots of peas and beans, if left in the soil, provide a rich store of nitrogen.

The usual rotation method for a small kitchen garden is to divide the area into three more or less equal plots. One of these plots should be manured the first year, the next plot manured the next year, and the last plot in the third year (see diagram). Plants that can be grown independently of such rotations include onions, which seem to do well in the same ground year after year, and herbs, which usually have an area of their own or may be grown in pots, tubs, or other containers. In very small gardens even rotations may not be able to prevent the spread of soil pests and diseases from one plot to the next. If this happens it may be desirable to exclude tomatoes, potatoes, or brassicas from your rotations, as these crops are especially vulnerable to attack by soil organisms. Tomatoes can be most successfully raised in grow bags, while brassicas and potatoes may be grown in large containers, provided the soil is replaced with fresh material every year. If container growing is not possible, you should make absolutely certain that your plots are free from soil pests before you incorporate these crops in the rotation again (*see* Brassicas, page 32).

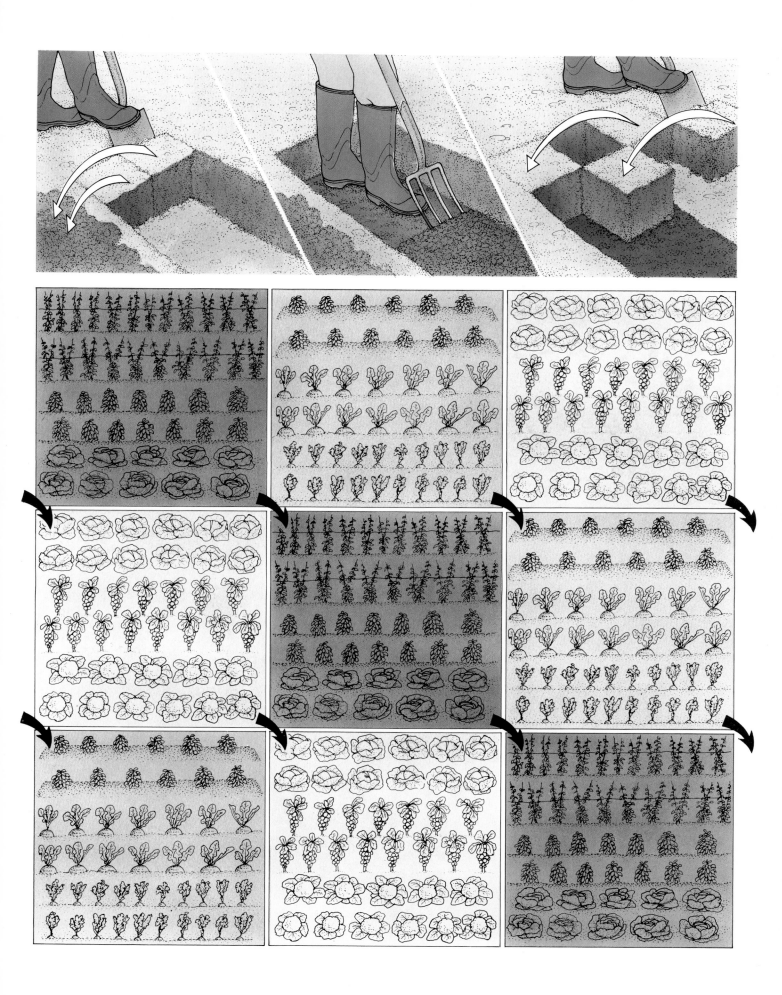

Planting and propagation

Before you devise your cropping programmes you will want to select one or more varieties of each crop. Recommended varieties of particular vegetables are given in Chapter 4, but you may well wish to try others as well. Narrowing down your choice may take several seasons of experimenting with different varieties. Most seed packets contain more seeds than you will require in any one season, so you can gradually assemble collections of different varieties, several of which can be grown in small quantities at the same time. Most seeds can be stored for several years if they are kept dry and cool. The best method is to store seed packets in a screw-top (air-tight) jar. Put a small quantity of silica gel in an open container in the bottom of the jar to absorb moisture, and keep the jar in a cool, dark place.

Sowing in the Main Plot

Prepare the plot for sowing by breaking down the dug-over soil a few weeks before sowing. Rake the soil backwards and forwards to knock down lumps, and remove debris and stones. Repeat the raking and clearing process a few days before sowing. The soil will need to be moist; if it is dry, water it a few days before sowing. Leave and do the same again a few hours before sowing.

Measure the rows, if necessary with a line and pegs, and draw them out to the correct depth for the plants in question using the edge of a rake, hoe, or other implement. Sow the seeds at the depths and intervals recommended in Chapter 4. Small seeds can be taken from the packet on the end of a plant label; large seeds can be planted in holes made with a dibber. Cover the seeds and water them in. Keep the soil moist, but not over-wet, during germination and after so that the plants can grow steadily without a check.

Indoor Sowing

Much-needed space in the kitchen garden can be saved by growing seeds indoors and planting them out later. The seeds may be sown individually in small pots (several of which can be placed in a large half-pot or other container); alternatively, they may be sown in seed trays. The growing medium is seed compost or

John Innes Compost No. 1, which should be moist but not soaking. After sowing, cover the seeds with a thin layer of compost and gently water them in. Place the pots or trays in large transparent polythene bags loosely held together at the top with a wide elastic band, string, or self-adhesive tape.

The polythene bags should be sited on a warm window sill, but do *not* place them in direct sunlight as this will quickly dry out the surface of the compost and may shrivel or burn the seedlings. When they emerge, the seedlings must be hardened off before they are planted out in the garden. The hardening-off process should be gradually intensified over a period of several weeks. Begin the process by opening the bags; then remove the bags altogether. Later, place the seedlings outdoors on sunny days, covering them with cloches or placing them in a frame at night. If neither cloches nor frame is available, bring the seedlings indoors at night and store them in the coolest part of the house.

In planting out the seedlings, take great care when removing them from their pots and trays to damage the roots as little as possible. Any compost clinging to the roots should be planted with the seedlings. Throughout the hardening-off period and when planting out, ensure that the growing medium is adequately moist.

Protection

Even after planting out, some of the more tender seedlings, such as marrows and squashes, will benefit from further protection for a week or two by covering them with cloches. You can also use cloches with some of the hardier crops, since by doing so you will bring forward their time of harvesting by a week or two; late-season tomatoes can also be bought forward in this way. Although glass cloches seem to have the best thermal and light-transmission properties, plastic ones have been greatly improved in recent years; moreover, they are lighter in weight and do not break so easily. Polythene 'tunnels' can be used instead of cloches. Whichever form you use, make sure it is anchored firmly to the soil.

Garden frames are, in a sense,

more substantial cloches (the heated types, in particular, have a variety of important uses). Like cloches they can be used to bring forward crops, such as lettuce; they are invaluable containers for the self-blanching of celery and for the more tender varieties of cucumbers, marrows, and squashes; and the heated types can be used for raising seedlings as well as for hardening them off later, when the amount of heat provided can be progressively lessened.

Seedling Diseases

The disease known as damping-off may affect some seedlings, particularly brassicas, which collapse on emerging. Cold, wet conditions are likely to be a cause of this. Dusting the seeds before sowing with thiram or captan may help to prevent an attack.

Mildews may also affect seedlings growing too closely together in wet soils, and some control may be achieved by applying zineb and thiram. Both diseases emphasise the importance of keeping the growing medium moist and well-drained rather than wet.

Cuttings

While sowing seed is the easiest way of propagating vegetable crops, you may need to use other methods for herbs. Seeds of French tarragon, for instance, are difficult to obtain, while those of rosemary do not always produce the particular variety required. For these and many other herbs, it is advisable to propagate from cuttings. The size of the individual cuttings taken depends on the species, but the technique is quite simple. The cuttings are grown in pots or trays, as for seeds. Special cutting composts are available, although John Innes

Tools and techniques: 1 Raking soil to break down surface for sowing. A fine tilth is important when you sow small seeds. 2 Drawing a V-shaped drill with the corner of a hoe. 3 Filling in a drill with the back of a rake. 4 Seedlings in peat pots packed in a large half-pot. 5 Levelling and firming compost in a seed box with a flat block of wood. 6 Seed box placed in a polythene bag tied at neck. 7–9 Three types of cloche. 10 Polythene tunnel. 11 Cold frame, useful (like cloches) for hardening-off seedlings. Easily fitted heating elements extend the uses of frames.

No. 1 or other soil-less composts are also quite suitable.

The cutting is sliced cleanly from the parent plant just below a leaf joint, using a sharp knife. Remove the lower leaves of the cutting to provide a bare stalk or stem to stick into the compost. Moisten the stem, shake off the surplus water, and insert the cut end into rooting powder. Make a small hole in the compost with a match stick or similar sized tool, and insert the cutting. Firm all around the cutting gently with finger tips, and water the cutting in. Enclose the pot or tray in a polythene bag, and thereafter use the same hardening-off procedure as for seedlings. Make sure that the leaves of the cutting do not touch the polythene bag or, later, the cloche, as this may cause them to develop a rot. During hardening off pinch out the top of the cutting; this will encourage the plant to develop side shoots, making for a bushier plant.

Propagators
A wide range of propagators in ready-made and kit forms is available for raising seeds and cuttings; or you can design and build your own. Their value lies in the fact that they provide controlled conditions of heat and humidity. Heat is provided either by cables or bulbs, the former being preferable as they distribute the heat more evenly. The more expensive models include a thermostat that can be pre-set to maintain the required temperature. If you plan regularly to raise plants indoors from seeds or cuttings a propagator, whether bought or made, could well prove to be a worthwhile investment.

Transplanting
The move from seed tray or pot to the soil of the kitchen garden can prove a difficult experience for a seedling, and the operation should be carried out gently and with great care. The results of careless transplanting may not become obvious for weeks or months: some plants may survive in a sickly condition; others may appear to grow well but will prove tough or poor-flavoured when harvested. Such failures can usually be avoided if you observe the following general rules:

1. Make sure the seedling is sufficiently hardened off before planting out.
2. Ensure that the soil it is growing in and in the main plot is moist (neither soggy nor dry).
3. Take care not to damage the seedling roots when removing them from the tray or pot; the roots should be partly or completely enclosed within a ball of compost.
4. If you are buying-in young plants (such as brassicas), rather than raising them from seeds, make sure that they do not dry out before you plant them. Unless they are to be planted out immediately after purchase (which is highly desirable), wrap them in several sheets of well-moistened newspaper.
5. When planting, make sure that the holes are both wider and deeper than the plant roots. Never try to cram the roots into a smaller than adequate hole. When the plant is in position, fill in the hole gently. The soil should be firm enough to prevent the plant from toppling over or from rocking in the wind, but if you pack it too tight you may deprive the roots of air and make it difficult for them to spread into the surrounding soil.
6. After planting, firm and water the plants in – again making sure not to over-soak the soil.

Planting out hardened-off bean seedlings. Take care not to damage the root balls. Firm in seedlings gently after filling in the soil.

RIGHT *Transplanting. 1 Make sure that the seedlings have been sufficiently hardened off. 2 Water the soil an hour or two before transplanting. 3 Invert a pot and gently tap out seedling, taking care to keep the root ball intact. Hold the seedling by the root ball when you plant it. 4 When in position the top of the root ball should be at or slightly below the level of the soil surface; the hole must be wide and deep enough not to cramp the ball. Carefully fill in soil around the root ball and then firm it in gently. 5 Water the seedling in; do not over-soak the soil.*

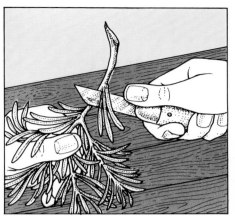

Propagating rosemary by cuttings. Slice off a twig from the parent plant with a clean, sharp knife. The cut should be just below a leaf node.

Remove leaves from the lower third of the cutting. This will provide a bare stalk or stem for insertion into the growing medium.

Moisten the lower end of the cutting, shake off surplus water, and insert the end into a rooting powder. This will promote root growth.

Dib holes with a match-stick and insert the cuttings. The medium can be special cutting compost or one of the other soil-less composts.

After gently firming in the cuttings with the finger tips, water them in. A 125 mm (5 in) pot will take four to six rosemary cuttings.

Enclose pot in a clear polythene bag, which should not touch the leaves. Place pot on a warm window sill out of direct sunlight.

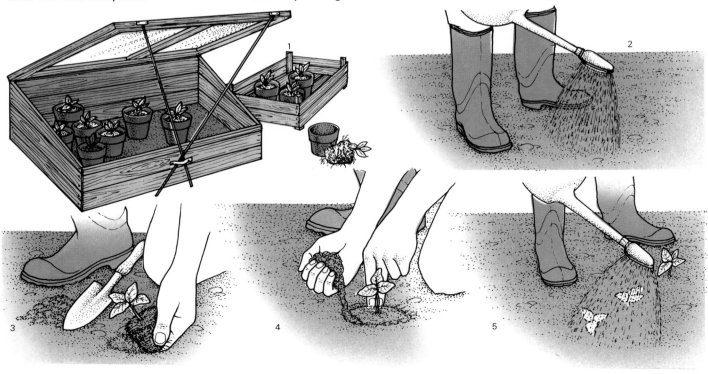

Vegetable crops

This chapter lists a selection in alphabetical order of familiar and not so familiar vegetables suitable for growing in the small kitchen garden. The notes include general remarks about each crop, soil requirements, cultivation technique, maintenance, harvesting, and (where appropriate) recommended varieties.

Pests and Diseases

Most vegetables are liable to attack by pests and diseases, although only a few are likely to prove a menace in the average kitchen garden. Some, such as slugs and mildews, can prove troublesome to crops in general, while others are specific to particular species or groups of crops. Where appropriate, remedies are given in the notes on the crop concerned. Chemical treatments for the control of pests and diseases are continuously being improved and the range available is now very great. Where possible, use a chemical that is specific to the particular pest or disease which is proving troublesome – but make sure that it is not harmful to the plant in question. Always apply the chemicals exactly according to the manufacturers' instructions. Remember that they are poisons: do not harvest or eat vegetables treated with them until the chemicals have lost their toxic properties (the waiting period will be given in the manufacturers' instructions for use); and keep the chemicals out of reach of children. Thoroughly wash all equipment, such as sprayers, cans, rubber gloves, and so on, that has come in contact with the chemicals.

Always keep your vegetable plot free of weeds, which not only consume soil nutriments earmarked for crops but may attract pests and diseases. Although many chemical weedkillers are available, in the small kitchen garden the best way to deal with weeds is to remove them by hand. Make sure to get rid of all their roots, and if possible complete your weeding before these undesirables have had time to set seed. Autumn debris, including the remains of harvested crops, also attracts pests and provides a breeding ground for diseases, so always make a point of clearing away any such unwanted vegetable matter. Much of it will be suitable for converting into compost.

Artichoke, Globe
Cynara scolymus

Globe artichokes make large plants and it might seem inappropriate to consider them for the small kitchen garden. However, the plant is so decorative, with its silvery foliage, that it may be grown with great effect in a herbaceous border and so relieve the pressure on space in the vegetable plot. If you are fond of globe artichokes it may well be worth your while growing them there, for they are expensive to buy.

Sow in a sunny position from about the middle of March in the south to May in the north. The earlier the sowing the better: if conditions are right, they will provide globes in their first year. The site should be well drained, with ample compost dug in. Allow the plants plenty of space: they grow to some 2 m (6½ ft) high, with a spread of about 1 m (3¼ ft). Plant 2 or 3 seeds in each site as an insurance against failure; if all the seeds germinate and grow in

each site, remove the weakest when they are a few inches high, leaving the best plants to grow on. If the plants are in a windy location, support them with bamboo stakes.

Subsequent attention is simple. Keep the soil free of weeds during the early weeks; thereafter the lower leaves will smother any weeds. The soil should be kept moist, and the plants fed occasionally with a dilute liquid fertiliser.

According to weather conditions and time of sowing, the globes will be ready from late June onwards. The edible parts of the globe artichoke are the bud scales and base. It is therefore essential to cut off the buds just before flowering, while they are tender. After you have removed the first bud from each plant, subsequent side buds may appear. Although tasty these will not be as large as the first bud unless you limit the number allowed to grow on each plant.

To maintain the quality of your

'Fuseau', with fairly smooth tubers, is one of the best Jerusalem artichokes.

crops, replace the plants every 3 years either by sowing fresh seed or by cutting suckers off the old plants. The suckers should be 250–300 mm (10–12 in) long, with some root attached, and should be cut in April and planted at once. You can also use the remains of the old plant to grow another crop – artichoke chards, which are used in the same way as Swiss chard. Cut the plants down to about 30 mm (1¼ in) in July. New growth will soon arise, and when it is about 600 mm (24 in) high bunch the leaves together and tie. Wrap them with strong paper and earth up the plants with dry soil to blanch the chards. The chards will be ready in about 6 or 7 weeks; after their removal the old plant should be composted. Globe artichokes are rarely troubled by pests or disease. The main problem is with slugs and snails, which enjoy the young growth and chards; they can be killed with Draza pellets.

Recommended variety 'Green Ball'

Site Sunny, open
Soil Well-drained, enriched
Sow Mid-March to May
Harvest Late June onwards

Artichoke, Jerusalem
Helianthus tuberosus

This plant can be used in two ways: raw in salads, and cooked by various methods. Like the globe artichoke, it is rather a large plant for the kitchen garden. Nor is it suitable for the herbaceous border, as it might be difficult to dig up the tubers without damaging flowering plants nearby. The best thing to do is to raise the plants in a corner of the garden where they can be used as a screen to hide your compost heap, dustbin, or other feature.

Plant the tubers in late winter or early spring, at a depth of 125–150 mm (5–6 in) and about 300–350 mm (12–14 in) apart. They will grow in virtually any soil, but do best with reasonable drainage and the addition of compost. Subsequently, keep the soil weed-free, and stake the plants

to keep them tidy. They may grow up to 3 m (10 ft) high and will get straggly in windy conditions unless you use stout poles or bamboo for staking; the plants can be secured by tying them with string or wire strung between the poles.

Harvesting is from late October onwards. Dig tubers as required, making sure to remove them all from each position during the course of the winter: they do not store well. Select small, well-formed tubers from the latest diggings for planting next year's crop. About 1 kg (2¼ lb) will be sufficient for a 5–6 m (16–20 ft) row.

Pests and diseases are unlikely to cause trouble.

Recommended variety 'Fuseau'

Site Anywhere, preferably with some sun
Soil Well-drained, enriched
Plant February–March
Harvest Late October onwards

Asparagus
Asparagus officinalis

Asparagus-growing calls for a good deal of patience; but it is an expensive delicacy to buy, and its decorative foliage adds charm to a herbaceous border. Many gardeners, however, set aside a small bed exclusively for asparagus because, once established, the plants will crop for many years.

You can raise asparagus from crowns or from seed, the former being the easier method. Either 1-year-old or 2-year-old crowns may be used: the 1-year-olds tend to establish themselves more readily, but they are not always easily available. The crowns should be planted as soon as possible after purchase in March to April: they may suffer irreparable damage if they begin to dry out. If you raise asparagus from seed it should be sown in a specially prepared seed bed in April. The seeds should be sown at a depth of 50 mm (2 in) in rows that are 300 mm (12 in) apart. In the summer thin out the plants so that they are about 150 mm (6 in) apart; keep them well watered in dry weather and weed-free. Asparagus plants are either male or

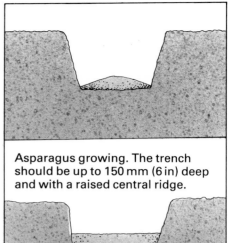

Asparagus growing. The trench should be up to 150 mm (6 in) deep and with a raised central ridge.

Place crown on the ridge, gently spreading out its radiating roots. Fill in the soil, firm it down, and water it.

Keep the asparagus bed weed-free; apply a general fertiliser annually from the second year.

Ideally, the first asparagus crop should be taken in the third year after planting.

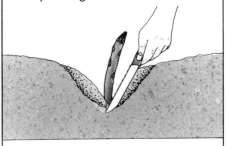

Shoots should be at least 100 mm (4 in) above soil before harvesting. Cut them 75 mm (3 in) below soil.

female, and healthy seedlings will flower in their first year. Male plants produce more shoots, so it is sensible to discard the females (you can tell the latter from their flowers or, later, their berries). Select the crowns from the remaining plants, and plant them out in March to April.

In a small garden three beds, either separate or as a part of a border approximately 1 m (3¼ ft) square, each containing 5 plants, should provide a good supply for two people; alternatively, the plants may be grown in rows 300 mm (12 in) apart with 300 mm between each plant.

Successful asparagus-growing depends greatly on careful preparation and cultivation of the bed. Double digging is strongly recommended because the plants develop deep roots; they also spread extensively, so the soil should be thoroughly cultivated to a distance of about 600 mm (24 in) around the bed. Dig the bed in the autumn. Add plenty of compost and other organic material such as leaf mould or, if possible, farmyard manure (if you live near the sea, well-rotted seaweed is even better). Leave the bed in a rough condition over the winter, then rake it level and clear debris and stones before spring planting. If you are using 1 m (3 ft) square beds, put one plant in the centre and the other four at each corner. Each hole should be 125–150 mm (5–6 in) deep, and wide enough to spread out the radiating roots. Then raise the centre of the hole so that the crown rests on a mound about 75–100 mm (3–4 in) below the surface of the bed. Fill in the soil, firming it gently. If you are planting in rows, take out a trench about 125–150 mm (5–6 in) deep and wide, mound the centre to a depth of 75–100 mm (3–4 in), and plant the crowns about 300 mm (12 in) apart along the ridge; fill in. Water the bed thoroughly after planting. Keep the beds weed-free, and apply a general fertiliser annually from the second year after planting.

Ideally you should wait until three years after planting before harvesting your first crop. However, the less-patient grower can take a few shoots, in May, two years after planting 1-year crowns, or only year after planting 2-year crowns. In subsequent years the weight of cropping may be increased. The shoots can be harvested when they show about 100 mm (4 in) above the ground; they should be cut with a sharp knife 75–100 mm (3–4 in) below the surface of the soil.

After harvesting the plants are allowed to grow on. In the autumn the foliage turns yellow and should be cut down and burnt before any berries have time to fall and give rise to unwanted seedlings. This is also the time to apply a mulch.

Asparagus plants suffer from various pests. Slugs may be killed with Draza pellets. The black-and-yellow asparagus beetle and its grey grub are often seen on the foliage and stems and can be dealt with by applying derris or malathion.

Recommended varieties
CROWNS 'Regal Pedigree'
SEED 'Martha Washington';
'Connovers Colossal'; 'Limburgia F₁'

Site Preferably sunny, fairly open but protected from wind
Soil Well-drained, with ample compost and other organic matter
Sow April
Plant March–April
Harvest April–May in first season; thereafter, April–June

Asparagus pea
Tetragonolobus purpureus

This plant is, in fact, neither a pea nor an asparagus, although it belongs to the pea family and its young, winged pods have a flavour resembling that of asparagus. With its mass of crimson pea-shaped flowers, the plant makes an attractive addition to the front of a border or small plot.

The plant prefers a sunny position and will grow in most soils except heavy clays, which should be lightened with sharp sand. Sow the seeds about 75 mm (3 in) apart and at a depth of about 12 mm (½ in); keep the soil weed-free and water it regularly during dry spells. The plants may grow about 400 mm (16 in) high and will look neater if supported with sticks and string.

The plants are harvested from late summer onward. Asparagus peas are often heavy croppers; the pods, which are eaten whole, should be picked when they are about 20–30 mm (¾–1¼ in) long; older pods tend to be tough.

Pests and diseases are rarely a trouble.

Site Preferably sunny
Soil Moist
Sow From late spring
Harvest Late summer onwards

Bean, Broad
Vicia faba

Easily grown and most useful because of its earliness, the broad bean is available in two main types, longpods and Windsors. The longpods, as the name implies, have longer pods, usually with more beans, which are of spherical shape; the Windsors have flatter beans, which are generally considered to be of better flavour. The types are further classified according to the colour of the bean skins, which may be white or green; the latter are better for freezing. Other variations are the early cultivars, such as 'Aquadulce', and the reddish-seeded 'Red Epicure', which is much liked by some for its taste. A number of dwarf varieties are also available.

Although broad beans are often sown in a double row, maximum cropping may be achieved by sowing the beans at intervals of 115 mm (4½ in) in single rows 450 mm (18 in) apart for taller varieties, and at intervals of 230 mm (9 in) in single rows 230 mm (9 in) apart for the dwarf varieties. The early 'Aquadulce' types are sown in October to November in the south and in January in the north; most other varieties are sown from February to April. If the weather is extremely cold it may be wise to delay sowing or alternatively to sow the beans in a garden frame and transplant them, after hardening off, when conditions improve. The dwarf variety 'The Sutton' may be sown under cloches in February; allow access for pollination by insects, and remove the cloches in late spring.

Broad beans need well-dug soil enriched with plenty of compost; however, on sites which were well prepared and manured for a previous crop, the addition of a general fertiliser may be sufficient. Do not apply fertilisers that are over-rich in nitrogen to the autumn-sown varieties as these will encourage too vigorous a growth in the young plants. Broad beans grow best in sunny locations, but they will tolerate some shade.

To ensure a tender crop, harvest the beans before the pods have fully developed – they should be 75–100 mm (3–4 in) long. If the crop is especially heavy, the young pods may be picked and cooked whole. After harvesting, cut down the stems and leaves but leave the roots in the soil: their concentration of nitrogen will benefit other crops.

A variety of diseases may affect broad beans. Slugs and snails may be dealt with by sprinkling Draza pellets. Blackfly may be discouraged by nipping out the growing point of the plants when plenty of flowers have developed and have started to set pods (these tops may be boiled and eaten too). You can control blackfly with insecticides such as dimethoate, but if you use them remember not to harvest and eat the beans until the chemicals have lost their toxicity. Chocolate spot, a disease that causes dark-brown spots on the plants, may occur especially on autumn-sown beans; well-drained soil helps to prevent it occurring, while spraying with Bordeaux mixture (a copper-based fungicide) may cure it.

Recommended varieties
EARLY 'Aquadulce Claudia'
GENERAL 'Imperial Green Longpod'; 'Masterpiece Green Longpod'; 'Green Windsor' varieties
RED 'Red Epicure', a longpod variety
DWARF 'The Sutton'; 'Bonny Lad'

Site Most places, not too shaded
Soil Enriched with compost, free-draining
Sow Earlies, October–January; others, February–April
Harvest Before beans are fully grown

Asparagus peas are easy to grow and crop well. The pods are eaten whole when they are no more than 20–25 mm (¾–1 in) long.

Bean, French
Phaseolus vulgaris

Now that fresh French beans have become something of a luxury, it is even more worthwhile growing your own. Dwarf and climbing forms are available, and both may be useful depending on the space you have available. There is a large number of dwarf varieties; you will obviously want to select for flavour and cropping ability, but within these categories it is well worth looking for the labour-saving stringless types. Most varieties have green pods; some are yellow, some are spotted, and others are purple (but turn dark green when cooked).

The beans can be sown in the main plot from March to April if they are protected with cloches which have been in position for a few weeks to warm the ground. Alternatively, they may be sown without protection from late April to May; these later dates should be followed in northern gardens and, in the south, if the weather is colder than usual. Owing to their size, the beans are easy to sow individually by dibbing holes 40–50 mm (1½–2 in) deep and about 100 mm (4 in) apart. After sowing, fill in the holes and lightly firm the soil. It is usual to sow in double, staggered rows, about 200–250 mm (8–10 in) apart, but blocks of plants may be sown with the same spacings to make beds 1·5–2 m (5–6½ ft) square using the dwarf varieties. Climbing varieties are sown at the same intervals but, as they will need the support of canes or netting to climb up, rows are more practical. Successional sowings at intervals of a few weeks will help to extend the cropping season. Sow a few extra beans at the row ends in case of failures, and transplant as necessary.

French beans will grow in a wide range of soils, but thrive best if the soil has been enriched the previous autumn with plenty of compost well dug in; they prefer a moist, sunny site. Keep the bed weed-free, and water it in dry weather. Crops planted early under cloches should be ventilated regularly until they are hardened off; the cloches should then be removed. Tunnel cloches are best for these crops.

Harvest as soon as the first pods are long enough to provide a meal; regular cropping encourages the development of more pods. After the harvest is over remove the plant stems and leaves but dig in the nitrogen-rich roots.

Usually disease-free, French beans are sometimes troubled by blackfly, which can be controlled with dimethoate or other insecticides.

Recommended varieties All the following are stringless and suitable for freezing; the colours refer to the pods
DWARF 'Flair', green, early; 'Kinghorn Wax', yellow, fine flavour; 'Pros Gitana', green, freeze whole; 'Royalty', purple, excellent flavour; 'Tendergreen', green, early
CLIMBING 'Blue Lake White Seeded', green, good flavour; 'Violet Podded Stringless', purple, fine flavour

Site Sunny
Soil Most types, enriched; moist
Sow March–April under cloches; late April–May unprotected
Harvest As soon as first beans ready; then regularly

Bean, Runner
Phaseolus coccineus

Runner beans are one of the most popular home-grown vegetables owing to the exceptionally fine flavour of a freshly picked young crop. In addition to the usual climbing forms, dwarf varieties are sometimes available and these are especially useful in a small garden where a tall screen of climbers might be inappropriate. A compact way of growing climbers is in the form of a wigwam or maypole, which may be made at home or bought and consists basically of twelve strings, wires, or bamboos radiating from the top of a stout stake inserted firmly in the ground. Whatever form of support is used, it should be fixed before sowing the beans. With double rows of poles or bamboos, tie the supports at the top to another pole laid horizontally. The pressure on supports may be considerable when the plants are cropping and the weather is windy.

Sow the beans individually, dib-bing them in 40–50 mm (1½–2 in) deep at intervals of 150 mm (6 in) from mid-May if the weather is favourable and there is no danger of frost. Cloche-protected beans can be sown in late April after the cloches have been in place for a few weeks to warm the soil. The seedlings can be ventilated in fine weather but do not remove the cloches until frosts are over. The rows should be about 600 mm (24 in) apart.

Runner beans repay good soil preparation. Choose a sunny site, not too exposed to wind. Double dig in autumn, mixing in plenty of compost; alternatively, dig a 450 mm (18 in) trench on the site of your rows and use it as a compost heap until early spring. Then remove most of the compost, thoroughly mix the rest with soil, and allow this to settle before sowing. Keep the soil well watered and weed-free after sowing. Pinch out the tops of climbing plants when they have reached the top of their supports. Sometimes the plants are inadequately pollinated and so produce fewer beans than normal. A number of growers believe that the white- or pink-flowered varieties suffer less in this way than the commoner scarlet types.

Harvest your crop when the pods are only a few inches long and before the seeds inside begin to press against the pod wall. Regular cropping extends fruitfulness.

Usually disease-free, runner beans may be infested with blackfly, which should be controlled with dimethoate or other insecticides.

Recommended varieties
'Achievement', suitable for freezing; 'Enorma', fine flavour, suitable for freezing; 'Fry', white flowered, nearly stringless and suitable for freezing; 'Red Knight', stringless, suitable for freezing; 'Sunset', pink flowered, fine flavour

Site Sunny, sheltered
Soil Well dug and enriched; moist
Sow Late April if protected; mid-May if unprotected
Harvest Regularly while pods are young and tender

A wigwam staking system is an easy-to-build and space-saving method of supporting your climbing runner beans.

Beetroot and Leaf Beet

Beta vulgaris

Beetroot and leaf beet are different forms of the same species. The yellow and white forms of beetroot also provide particularly good foliage for food, so this is a true double crop. Beetroots vary in shape; the globe forms are the most popular nowadays, but the long and intermediate types are better for storing through the winter. Globe beets are less likely to bolt – that is, run to seed and develop tough roots. Besides the leaf beet known as perpetual spinach, another leaf-beet form has the central leaf vein developed into a thick midrib; it is called Swiss chard, silver, or seakale beet if the veins are white, and rhubarb chard or beet (or ruby chard) if the veins are reddish crimson. The rib of these varieties is often cooked separately from the leafy part, which may also be used as spinach.

Beetroot

Most varieties of beetroot have several seeds in a cluster; this must be sown whole, but it will need thinning later. Some modern types, however, are single-seeded. The seeds or seed clusters are large enough to sow individually and should be planted in rows or blocks from late March to July, the later sowing applying particularly to the long varieties intended for winter storage. All varieties should be sown at a depth of about 20 mm (¾ in), with rows 180–300 mm (7–12 in) apart. The globe varieties should be sown at 100 mm (4 in) intervals, the long varieties at 150 mm (6 in).

Beetroot grows on light or heavy soils that have been enriched the previous autumn with well-rotted compost; do *not* use fresh manure. The ideal is soil that was used for a well-manured crop the previous season; it should be topped-up with a general fertiliser applied two weeks before sowing. When the seedlings become established they can be thin-

ned to one per sowing point. Keep the soil free of weeds.

Globe varieties should be harvested when young, usually from June onwards. It is best to twist off, rather than cut, the tops of red beet, which otherwise may 'bleed'; the tops of yellow and white varieties, however, may be removed with a sharp knife. Long varieties may be left to develop and pulled in early winter, but it may be necessary to protect the late-pulled crop against frost by covering the soil with straw. The beet may be stored in boxes of sand in a frost-free shed or in a clamp in the open. Before storing examine each root carefully; diseased or damaged ones must be discarded as they may rot the others. Remove the tops and soil from the roots before storing.

The leaves of young beetroot may be burrowed into by maggots of the mangold fly. Treat by spraying with dimethoate or trichlorphon. Slugs and snails should be kept at bay with Draza pellets.

Recommended varieties

GLOBE 'Avonearly', good for early sowings, very slow to bolt; 'Boltardy', good for early sowings, slow to bolt; 'Burpee's Golden', yellow-rooted, sweet, tasty leaves for 'spinach'; Detroit 'Little Ball', small globes, excellent quality, useful for late sowing and pickling; 'Monodet', single-seeded; 'Snowhite', white-rooted, sweet, good 'spinach' leaves
LONG 'Cheltenham Green Top', broad-topped; 'Cheltenham Mono', single-seeded; 'Cylindra' ('Housewives Choice'), cylindrical; Long Blood Red 'Covent Garden', small-topped

Leaf beet

These forms of beet are grown for their leaves only, the roots being of no value. The Swiss chard types and 'Rhubarb Chard' are very decorative, particularly the latter, and may be grown as attractive additions to the ornamental part of the garden. Sow from April onwards. Seeds may be sown individually at a depth of 20–25 mm (¾–1 in); if planted in rows, sow seeds at intervals of 200–250 mm (8–10 in), with rows about 450 mm (18 in) apart.

A productive vegetable plot. Inset: 'Burpee's Golden', a yellow-rooted globe beetroot; its tasty leaves can be used as spinach.

Brassica disease and pests. Club root, a fungal disease, thrives in wet, acid soils. Above-ground symptoms are distorted, bluish stems and leaves.

Small cabbage-white butterfly larvae eat brassica leaves. The eggs (usually on the underside of leaves) and larvae can be controlled with derris.

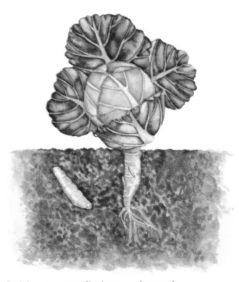

Cabbage-root fly larvae (greatly enlarged here) tunnel into roots of transplanted seedlings. Discourage them by mixing bromophos with soil before transplanting.

The soil should be well prepared in the autumn, with plenty of compost dug in. After sowing keep the soil weed-free, and moist in dry weather.

The crop can be harvested as required as soon as the leaves are large enough; do not remove all the leaves of a plant at the same time. The leaves of the chard varieties should be pulled off; those of 'Perpetual Spinach' should be cut.

Protect against pests as for beetroot.

Recommended varieties 'Lucullus' (Swiss chard), large leaves; 'Perpetual Spinach'; 'Rhubarb Chard', a red form of Swiss chard; 'Silver' or 'Seakale' beet (Swiss chard)

Site Open, with not too much shade
Soil Most types; do not use fresh manure for root-beet soils
Sow Beetroot, late March onwards; leaf beet, April onwards
Harvest As required, when growth is sufficient

Borecole *see* Kale

Brassicas

The term 'brassica' is usually taken to refer to members of the botanic genus *Brassica*. Most of these are grown for their leaves and flower heads: sprouting and winter broccoli, Brussels sprouts, cabbages and savoys, cauliflowers, and kale. Other members of the genus include swedes and turnips, which are grown for their fleshy roots, and kohlrabi, grown for its swollen stem. The genus *Brassica* belongs to the family of plants known as the Cruciferae, which also includes another popular vegetable, the radish, as well as many familiar flowering plants. The vegetables are dealt with individually in alphabetical order, but this is a good place to have a word about some of the more common pests and diseases that attack most of the brassicas grown for their leaves and flower heads.

One of the most serious pests of this group of vegetables are the larvae of the cabbage-root fly, which are especially damaging to newly transplanted seedlings. The larvae tunnel into the roots of the young plants, causing them to wilt. The best way to control attacks is to sprinkle bromophos powder into the soil when the seedlings are transplanted.

Club root (also known as finger-and-toe) is a fungal disease that damages, and may destroy, the roots by causing them to swell. An outbreak of club root can be recognised by its effect on the stem and leaves, which become distorted and may turn a bluish colour. The disease may be controlled with thiophanate-methyl (available as Murphy Club Root Dip) and also by careful cultivation of the soil. Club root thrives chiefly in wet, acid soils. Wetness can be prevented by improving soil drainage by means of thorough digging and the addition of sharp sand and peat. Acidity can be reduced by digging in hydrated lime: about 1 kg per 2 m^2 (1 lb per 10 sq ft) in the first year and about half as much in subsequent years. As an added precaution, dip the roots of the seedlings in a paste of calomel dust and water when you are transplanting them.

These nuisances are the best possible reasons for including brassicas in your rotation system. Both pests and diseases will build up if brassicas are planted in the same soil for several years in succession.

Caterpillars, mainly the larvae of the cabbage white butterflies, are a familiar pest of brassicas and can severely damage the leaves. They can be removed by hand, but a better method is to destroy the eggs (usually on the underside of leaves) before they hatch. Among chemical controls of both eggs and larvae, derris is the safest; it will also kill the flea beetle, which eats small holes in brassica leaves.

Broccoli and Cauliflower
Brassica oleracea varieties

This species name includes many varieties of brassica that bear tasty flowerheads and stalks. It might be thought that, because many of these plants need a good deal of elbow room and take rather a long time to mature, they would hardly qualify for a place in the small kitchen garden. In fact, careful planning and selection of varieties will enable you to choose types eminently suited to any kitchen garden; moreover, the range as a whole adds up to a species that can be harvested in every month of the year. To give you some idea of the possibilities, the calabrese type of green sprouting broccoli is sown in early summer and cropped in the autumn; mini-cauliflowers need to be spaced only 150 mm (6 in) apart; and catch crops such as quick-maturing lettuce are quite content to grow in the spaces between the normal cauliflowers.

The main varieties of broccoli can be divided into three groups: sprouting broccoli, which has loose clusters of flowerheads; the green calabrese type, which is harvested in summer and autumn; and the more curd-like purple- and white-headed types, which are harvested in winter and spring. Winter cauliflower (which used to be called 'broccoli') is similar to the summer form but the curds may be slightly coarser and of deeper colour; it is harvested from early winter to mid-summer. Summer cauliflower (usually called just 'cauliflower') is in fact harvestable from early summer to late winter according to type.

Calabrese broccoli and mini-

'Purple Cape' is a winter cauliflower with good-quality purple curds. It is harvested in February or March.

Broccolis and cauliflowers offer a range that can be cropped throughout the year. Purple sprouting broccolis (as here) are ready for harvesting from March until May, depending on variety.

Green sprouting broccolis, also known as calabrese, are mainly quick-growing types that are sown in June or July (preferably under cloches) and are harvested from August to November.

Mini-cauliflowers, like calabrese, are sown where they are to grow. The early types are harvested in July and the late ones from October onwards.

cauliflower are sown in the main plot, the broccoli in June and July, the mini-cauliflower in successional sowings from early April onwards. Sow two or three seeds at each growing point at a depth of 20–25 mm (¾–1 in). The calabrese should be sown in blocks, at intervals of 150 mm (6 in) in one direction, and 300 mm (12 in) in the other; mini-cauliflower should be 150 mm apart in each direction. Both types will crop earlier if they are protected with cloches, which should be positioned two weeks before sowing.

All other broccoli and cauliflower should be sown in a seed bed and planted out later. They are sown at a depth of 20–25 mm (¾–1 in) and, when seedlings show, are thinned out to intervals of 250 mm (10 in). The broccoli and winter cauliflower are sown in mid-April to mid-May; the summer cauliflower is sown in March and April for summer harvesting, and in April to mid-May for autumn and later harvesting. The seedlings are transplanted when they have developed two or three true leaves. Water the seed bed first, then lift the seedlings so that they retain as much soil as possible; transfer them immediately to the main plot, firm them in, and water. Seedlings should be planted 600 mm (24 in) apart in rows or blocks; an exception is 'Nine Star Perennial', which will crop for several years if all its heads are harvested, and should be planted at intervals of 900 mm (36 in). Handle the seedlings as gently as possible, and make sure they are planted out at the same depth as they were in the seed bed.

For all the sprouting broccolis and winter cauliflower the soil should *not* be dug over after the previous crop has been harvested, but a low-nitrogen fertiliser should be raked or hoed in before planting. The site should be open but full sun is not essential; keep the soil free of weeds.

For summer cauliflower the soil should be dug over, preferably some months before planting, and plenty of compost incorporated (manure if you can get it). Break down the soil clods, firm by trampling over the site, and add a sprinkling of general fertiliser before planting. Site as for broccoli. Keep weed-free and feed slow-growing summer varieties (but *not*

winter cauliflower) with a high-nitrogen fertiliser. Protect heads from yellowing in strong sun by folding the leaves over the curds.

For the main pests and diseases, *see* Brassicas.

Each variety is harvested as it becomes ready, before the flowers open. After the main head of sprouting varieties is cut, small side heads should form. Ripe cauliflower curds soon deteriorate in warm weather, so inspect them regularly as they approach maturity. They should be harvested early in the morning before they are heated by the sun.

Recommended varieties The following are among the best of each type available; harvesting times are in parentheses
SPROUTING BROCCOLI, GREEN OR CALABRESE (all suitable for freezing) 'Express Corona' F$_1$ (August to September); 'Corvet', F$_1$ (about 2 weeks after 'Express Corona'); 'Autumn Spear' (September to November)
SPROUTING BROCCOLI, PURPLE AND WHITE (all suitable for freezing) 'Early Purple Sprouting' (March to April); 'Late Purple Sprouting' (April to May); 'Early White Sprouting' (March); 'Late White Sprouting' (April)
SPROUTING BROCCOLI, PERENNIAL 'Nine Star Perennial' (March to April)
WINTER CAULIFLOWER: 'Angers' varieties (January to June); 'English Winter' varieties (April to June); 'Purple Cape', has a purple curd (February to March); 'Walcheren Winter' varieties, fine white heads (April and May)
SUMMER CAULIFLOWER 'All the Year Round' (matures over a long period according to sowing date); 'Barrier Reef', compact (late October); 'Canberra' (October to November); 'Dominant' (June to July); 'Kangaroo' (September to October)
MINI-CAULIFLOWER 'Garant' (from July); 'Predominant' (September to November)

Site Preferably open
Soil Must be well-drained and alkaline (*see* Brassicas)
Sow Most varieties, spring; calabrese, early summer
Harvest Most of the year, depending on variety

Brussels Sprout
Brassica oleracea gemmifera

Like other brassicas, Brussels sprouts tend to occupy rather a lot of space in the small kitchen garden, but (as with cauliflowers) you can economise on space by raising catch crops between the individual plants. Sprout varieties enable the crop to be harvested over a long period. If you are reluctant to devote precious space to these crops for the entire growing season, you may be able to club together with a friend or neighbour, so that each of you grows varieties maturing at different times.

Sow in a seed bed from March to April and transplant about 8–10 weeks later in a plot prepared as for purple and white broccoli. Plant ordinary varieties up to 900 mm (36 in) apart, and the newer medium to dwarf types 500 mm (20 in) apart. Alternatively the ground may be dug, allowed to settle, and then trampled well in advance of planting (firm but not hard ground is essential for firm sprouts). Earlier seedlings may be raised under the protection of cloches. Young plants may also be bought and planted out immediately.

Pests and diseases: *see* Brassicas.

Harvest the sprouts as soon as they are ready by snapping off each head individually with a downward movement. Pick the lowest ones first. Remove any dead or decaying leaves and poor-quality sprouts immediately. When all the sprouts have been removed from a plant, its top cluster of leaves may be used as greens.

Recommended varieties 'Citadel', F_1, medium height, suitable for freezing, ready December onwards; 'Fasolt', F_1, medium to tall, suitable for freezing, crops into February; 'Peer Gynt', F_1, very popular, medium dwarf, suitable for freezing, matures September onwards; 'Rubine', attractive red sprouts of good quality

Site Open
Soil Firm, well-composted
Sow March to April, or earlier under cloches
Harvest September onwards

A justly popular Brussels sprout, 'Peer Gynt' is one of the earlier varieties.

Cabbage, including Savoy

Brassica oleracea capitata

This is another versatile brassica whose varieties give crops throughout the year, and it is quite suitable for small gardens if grown with intercrops. Of special interest for small gardens is the variety 'Minicole', an F_1 hybrid which may be grown more closely spaced than ordinary types.

There are four main seasonal groups of cabbage: spring-sown for use in summer and autumn; summer-sown for use in autumn and winter; autumn-sown for use in spring; late-spring-sown Savoy cabbages for use in autumn and winter. If pressure on space is particularly severe, the autumn-sown varieties may be especially useful to you because they can be harvested and cleared from the plot before your spring and summer plantings of other vegetables get under way.

There is some overlap and flexibility in the times of sowing listed above, and some varieties may be used in several groups. All groups should be sown, like purple and white broccoli, in a prepared seed bed and transplanted later. The spring-sown varieties are usually sown in March and April and may require protection in a frame or under cloches in the north or if the weather is colder than usual; in the south they may be sown earlier if protected in this way. Transplant when two or three true leaves have developed and make sure that no check is given by watering the soil beforehand. Space 'Minicole' about 250 mm (10 in) apart in rows or blocks, compact varieties such as 'Hispi' 350–400 mm (14–16 in) apart, and others 450 mm (18 in) apart. The ground should have been well prepared beforehand, with plenty of compost incorporated.

The summer-sown (May to June), autumn-sown (late-July to August) and Savoy varieties are in due course similarly transplanted, but to a bed which was prepared with compost for the previous crop. Space the transplants 450–500 mm (18–20 in) apart in rows or blocks. Water the soil in dry weather and keep it weed-free at all times.

Autumn-sown cabbages may also be used to provide spring greens. If you wish to try this, transplant to half the spacings given above; blocks may be converted to short rows by close planting along the width or along the length only. When the greens are mature, remove every *second* plant; this will leave the original spacing for the remaining cabbages to heart up later in the normal way.

Some varieties, such as 'Holland Late Winter', are sown in April, cut or pulled up in November, and may then be stored over winter in a cool and airy shed after any damaged outer leaves have been removed.

Red cabbage is sown in spring in the south; in the north it should be sown in late summer and over-wintered as seedlings under cloches or in frames. Transplant spring-sown varieties as usual, and late-summer sowings in the spring; allow a spacing of 600 mm (2 ft) in rows or blocks. Red cabbage is a versatile crop as it can be eaten raw, cooked, or pickled.

Pests and diseases: *see* Brassicas.

Recommended varieties

SPRING-SOWN 'Greyhound', short, small, pointed, reliable variety; 'Hidena', F_1, round, may be pulled up complete for storage; 'Hispi', F_1, compact, pointed, may be also autumn-sown and overwintered under protection; 'Holland Late Winter', 'Holland Winter E.40' (Langendijk 3), late, may be cut for storage; 'Minicole', F_1, small, round, long-standing, may be closely grown; 'Niggerhead' ('Red Drumhead'), large, red; 'Ruby Ball', F_1, red, excellent quality; 'Vienna' ('Babyhead'), compact, small, round, stands well, good quality

SPRING-SOWN SAVOY 'Alexanders No 1', large, late – harvests well into spring; 'Best of All', large, early – ready in autumn; 'Celtic', F_1 (a hybrid with a cabbage), hardy, late-winter; 'January Prince' (a selection of 'January King'), small, hardy, autumn to winter; 'Savoy King', large, light-green, autumn

SUMMER-SOWN 'Christmas Drumhead', compact, round, late autumn to early winter; 'Winnigstadt', compact, pointed, autumn

AUTUMN-SOWN 'April', compact, pointed, ready from April; 'Offenham Flower of Spring', large heads, ready April to May; 'Wheeler's Imperial', compact, pointed, ready April to May

Site Preferably open
Soil Well drained
Sow According to variety
Harvest According to variety

Ideal for the small plot, 'Minicole' cabbage is spaced only 250 mm (10 in) apart.

Cabbage, chinese
Brassica chinensis pekinensis

This vegetable, which is rapidly gaining in popularity, is especially useful to the gardener with little space, for it may be cooked as an ordinary cabbage or eaten raw with salads instead of lettuce. Owing to its late sowing time and speedy growth it may be used as a catch crop after clearing an earlier crop.

Sow, in late June or July, two or three seeds at each growing point at a depth of 12 mm (½ in) and at intervals of 300 mm (12 in). When the seedlings emerge, thin to the best individual at each growing point. The plants can alternatively be sown fewer at a time and successively to achieve harvesting over a longer period. But do not sow too early or the plants may bolt.

Chinese cabbage grows best on an open site that receives shade from mid-afternoon onwards. If you are not sowing in soil enriched for the previous crop, dig in plenty of compost in the spring; then scatter on a general fertiliser before sowing. Bolting may also be caused by lack of moisture, so keep the soil well watered and weed free.

'Sampan', an F₁ hybrid, is one of the best of the Chinese cabbages.

Harvesting is in late autumn: the plants take only about two months to reach maturity.

Recommended varieties 'Nagoaka', F₁, early, tall, cos-shaped; 'Sampan', F₁, conical, slow to bolt; 'Tip Top', F₁, later than 'Nagoaka', and shorter; 'Wong Bok', late

Site Open, shaded later in the day
Soil Good
Sow June to July
Harvest Late autumn

Carrot

Daucus carota sativa

The carrot is a splendid vegetable for small gardens or for growing in tubs and other large containers. In containers the soil mixture can easily be controlled, and even in small, odd patches of ground it is not much trouble to provide the stone-free, light, but rich soil in which carrots thrive. Some varieties are recommended for growing on shallow soils; but as the only reason for this is

Celeriac, an excellent salad vegetable, needs plenty of moisture to thrive. Remove the lower leaves as they turn yellow.

their short length (or roundness, as in the 'Early French Frame' type), it is a better proposition to prepare your planting site well and get a decent-sized carrot out of it. Carrots are classified, according to root shape and size, as stump-rooted, long, intermediate, and so on. The short, stump-rooted varieties are useful for early crops, usually brought forward by protection under a cloche or in a cold frame; the lighter the soil, the longer the carrot type that may be grown. (Strange-shaped carrots sometimes make the headlines; their formation is usually due either to the root striking a stone or to the use of too-fresh manure.)

Sow in warmer areas from March

onwards (or from February if protection is provided) and in colder ones from April. The seeds are large enough to handle individually, and in small plots this is worth doing. Sow a few at a time at intervals of about 3 weeks so as to get a succession of carrots; they should be sown, in rows or blocks, at a depth of 12–20 mm (½–¾ in) and 100–150 mm (4–6) apart depending on root type.

Light soil should be improved by the addition of peat and very-well-matured compost dug in as early as possible in the autumn. Heavier soils can be used if they have been well composted for a previous crop; but they should also be dug in the autumn and lightened with the

addition of peat and sharp sand. Soil for half-tubs or other deep containers may be prepared on the above principles; but it may be easier to buy prepared soil, such as John Innes 2 or 3, and 'improve' it with sharp sand and peat in proportions of 7 parts prepared soil, 2–3 parts peat, and 1 part sharp sand. Then sprinkle on a dusting of general fertiliser and fork it in. Leave the soil for a month, keeping it moist if the weather is unexpectedly dry.

If the seeds were sown thinly enough, no thinning will be necessary when the seedlings emerge. If more than one seedling emerges from a single growing point, retain only the strongest one and firm the soil again. Remove the unwanted plants from the site as the scent of crushed foliage attracts the carrot-root fly. When the seedlings are 40–50 mm (1½–2 in) high, heap a little soil around the root; this will help prevent development of green-topped roots.

The carrot-root fly is the major pest of carrots. Its grubs burrow into the roots and ruin them. They can be controlled to some extent with bromophos or other suitable insecticides, which should be sprinkled into the soil when sowing.

Harvest as required. A surplus of the larger-rooted varieties may be pulled in late autumn and early winter for storing in boxes of sand kept in a cool but frost-free shed. Cut off the leaves before boxing.

Recommended varieties (all suitable for freezing) 'Amsterdam Forcing' (selected strains such as 'Amstel' and 'Sweetheart'), stump-rooted, early, suitable for forcing; 'Chantenay Red Cored' (selected strains such as 'Royal Chantenay' and 'Supreme'), stump-rooted, main crop; 'Guerande' ('Oxheart'), large-shouldered, stump-rooted variety suitable for forcing, fine flavour; 'Juared' ('Juwarot'), excellent flavour, suitable for storing; 'Nantes' (selected strains such as 'Express' and 'Tiptop'), suitable for early, late, and forcing

Site Not too shady
Soil Light, stone-free, rich
Sow From March in the open; from February if protected
Harvest When required

Cauliflower *see* Broccoli and Cauliflower

Celeriac
Apium graveolens rapaceum

Derived from the wild celery plant, celeriac (or turnip-rooted celery) is quite easy to grow provided the ground is richly prepared and plenty of moisture is available during its growing season; if checked through lack of moisture celeriac is liable to bolt (run to seed) and produce hard, stringy roots. If you like the rooty bit of ordinary celery but have not tried celeriac, a small block may provide a welcome late-autumn and winter vegetable, delicious raw in salads or cooked.

Sow, in late May or early June, in rows or blocks, about 300 mm (12 in) apart, carefully tapping only two or three seeds out at each point, and just cover the seeds with soil. When the seedlings appear, thin them to the strongest at each growing point. Alternatively, sow seeds in half pots indoors in late March and plant out in May after hardening them off in a cold frame or under a cloche. A recent introduction, 'Jose', is especially suitable for small gardens because it can be spaced at about half the distance needed for the other varieties.

Celeriac needs a sunny or very lightly shaded site and a deep, rich, well-drained soil. The soil should be dug in the winter, with a good quantity of well-rotted compost (or, preferably, manure) thoroughly mixed in. Before sowing, dress the soil with a high-nitrogen fertiliser. Never allow the soil to dry out, and keep it weed-free. Remove the plants' lower leaves as they begin to yellow.

Harvest the crop as required from late September to November. Surplus roots may be stored in boxes of sand or peat in a frost-free place or earthed up where they are until required.

Celeriac occasionally suffers from leaf miners, which should be dealt with by systemic insecticides based on dimethoate, malathion, or combinations of the two, or by pinching the blister mines.

Recommended varieties 'Globus', fine flavour; 'Jose', close-spaced; 'Iram', does not discolour on cooking, stores well; 'Marble Ball', well-flavoured, solid

Site Open
Soil Enriched, well-drained but moisture-retentive
Sow Indoors, from March; outdoors, late-May to June
Harvest Autumn

Celery
Apium graveolens dulce

The old varieties of trenched celery are too demanding of space for growing in small kitchen gardens. But self-blanching celery may be grown in fairly compact blocks in the open, in cold frames, or even in tubs or other large containers.

Sow in late May or early June in blocks, with about 230 mm (9 in) space between growing points. Alternatively they can be sown indoors in a seed tray in mid-March; do not cover the seeds in the tray with compost, but make sure they do not dry out during germination. The seedlings can be transplanted, after hardening off, in late May: they may be planted out in the main plot or in a cold frame; the protection offered by the latter ensures that the seedlings will not suffer a check when they are removed from the seed tray.

Celery needs a rich, well-drained but moisture-retentive soil, preferably slightly acid. If it is to be grown in the main plot, dig the ground thoroughly in the winter, mixing in well-rotted compost or, preferably, manure. Blanching is improved by limiting the amount of light getting to the edible petioles (stems); if the celery is growing in the open, surround the outer plants in the block with a bank of soil or straw; if in tubs, the surface of the growing medium should be well below the rim; if in a cold frame, the walls of the frame will be sufficient to promote blanching. Keep the soil moist at all times, and weed it frequently as weeds can easily smother the young plants.

Celery is likely to suffer from various pests and diseases. One of the most serious can be avoided if you ensure that you buy only seed that has been treated for leaf-spot fungus. Leaf miners can be controlled as for celeriac. Slugs and snails can be dealt with by sprinkling Draza pellets around the plants.

Recommended varieties 'Golden Self Blanching' and its selection 'Mammoth Self Blanching', dwarf and compact; 'Lathom Self Blanching', compact, slow to bolt

Site Suitable for blocks, or plant in frames or tubs
Soil Enriched, well-drained but moisture-retentive
Sow indoors, from March; outdoors, late May to June
Harvest Late summer and early autumn

Chard *see* Beet, Leaf

Chicory and Endive
Cichorium intybus **and** *C. endivia*

Many people confuse these two salad plants, so it is sensible to deal with them together; they are, in fact, closely related, and in some cultivated forms they are quite similar in appearance.

Chicory is grown in two main forms: the forced 'chicons' (blanched hearts) known as Witloof or Brussels chicory, and the leafy forms resembling cos lettuce. Endive produces the familiar curly salad leaves. With the exception of the Witloof type, cultural conditions are the same for chicory and endive apart from their sowing times. All are usually untroubled by pests or diseases, although protection against slugs and snails is advisable.

Witloof Chicory
Great improvements have been made to this type in recent years and, although many seedsmen still sell the old type which needs covering with soil when the chicons are being produced, the cultural directions given here apply to the new, easier-to-grow varieties recommended below.

Sow the seed in blocks in April to June. The seeds, two or three to each growing point, should be sown at a depth of about 12 mm (½ in) and about 150–200 mm (6–8 in) apart. The seedlings should later be thinned to the strongest at each point.

The soil should be deep and fertile – preferably a plot that was well-composted for the previous crop. Witloof chicory is an acid-hater, so add lime to the soil if necessary. A slightly acid soil will require about 160 g/m² (about 5 oz per 10 sq ft) of lime, which should be well worked in the previous autumn. An open but not necessarily very sunny site is suitable. Water the soil in dry weather and keep it clear of weeds at all times. Remove any flower shoots.

The roots are dug up from about mid-October for chicon production. Take the required number, cut off the leaves 12 mm (½ in) above the crown, and trim the root ends. The roots should be up to 300 mm (12 in) long and about 75 mm (3 in) in diameter; discard thin, damaged, or forked examples. Forcing is done in deep boxes or pots containing peat or sandy soil. The roots are packed vertically, 40–50 mm (1½–2 in) apart, with their crowns about 25 mm (1 in) above the surface of the soil. Water them in gently, and then cover the boxes or pots with inverted ones of the same size so that the crowns are in complete darkness. Store at a temperature of 10–13°C (50–56°F).

It is vital to exclude all light, but the 'hearts' (chicons) should be examined every so often and the soil kept moist. The crop will be ready in three to four weeks, depending on the temperature. Repeat the operation at intervals, according to your needs. After the leaves have been cropped the roots can be planted again in the spring. Plants not lifted for forcing may be earthed up, covered with about 200 mm (8 in) of soil, for later outdoor-grown chicons.

Other Chicories and Endive
Sow chicories from mid-June to mid-July as for Witloof, but 250–300 mm (10–12 in) apart, and endive from July to September 300 mm (12 in) apart. If an extended cropping period is required, sow successively.

Soil and site requirements are as for Witloof. If the site was not pre-

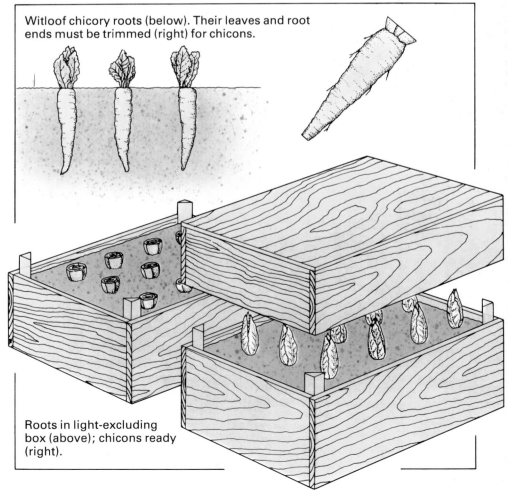

Witloof chicory roots (below). Their leaves and root ends must be trimmed (right) for chicons.

Roots in light-excluding box (above); chicons ready (right).

pared with compost for a previous crop it should be improved by the addition of compost dug in well before sowing and allowed to settle. Just before sowing rake in a light dressing of a general fertiliser.

The modern varieties of chicory, as recommended below, grow like cos lettuce and need no blanching; they are harvested in late autumn and winter. You should begin blanching endives from September, about three weeks before they are required, by covering them with a large light-excluding pot or box. Blanch a few at a time, as they do not keep well.

Recommended varieties
WITLOOF 'Normato', early, forcing to December; 'Mitado', mid-season, forcing to February; 'Tardivo', late, forcing late-winter to spring
OTHER CHICORIES 'Crystal Head' or 'Snowflake'; 'Sugar Loaf' ('Pain de Sucre'); 'Winter Fare'
ENDIVES 'Batavian Green' ('Batavian Broad Leaved'), for autumn and winter; 'Green Curled' ('Moss

Endive 'Batavian Green' is ready for harvesting in autumn and winter.

Curled'), for late summer and autumn

Site Open
Soil Good, not acid
Sow Witloof, April–June; other chicory, mid-June–mid-July; endives, July–September.
Harvest Witloof, from mid-October; other chicory, late autumn–winter; endives, September onwards

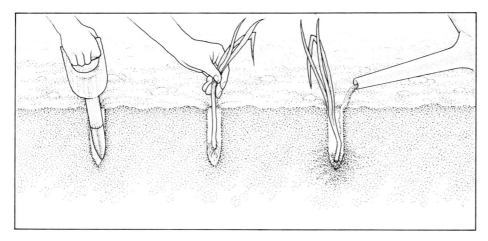

Watering in leeks after dibbing a 150 mm (6 in) hole.

Firming in a transplanted seedling.

Newly lifted onions left to dry on soil.

Possible layout for a small garden. At extreme left, below wall, are herbs – dill at top, sage and thyme at bottom, bay in tub. To the right, in borders, are (from top) beetroot, carrots, and globe artichoke; above hose-reel is a rosemary bush. Middle plot (left to right): sprouts, cabbage, savoys, curly kale, turnips, celeriac, potatoes. Right-hand plot (left to right): netted peas, lettuce, radishes, dwarf peas, leeks, dwarf French beans, onions, runner beans trained up wigwams; marrows under cloche. Below path at bottom (left to right) staking tomatoes, two bush tomatoes, continental staking tomatoes – all in grow bags. At top right are two compost bins beside shed. Not all of these crops, of course, would be growing at the same time.

Corn Salad
Valerianella locusta

Corn salad, also known as lamb's lettuce, is a hardy, low-growing, broad-leaved annual. It provides a useful substitute for lettuce in early spring and from autumn to winter, and it may be cropped through summer, by successional sowings.

Sown in early autumn, the plants will provide leaves later in autumn and (under cloches) in winter. Sown in late winter (under cloches) to spring it will provide crops in spring and early summer. Sow the seeds in the main plot spaced 75–100 mm (3–4 in) apart in a small group or groups; cover them with a light sprinkling of soil and water lightly. Thin out to one plant per growing point if two or more seeds germinate at any one point. It may also be grown in pots or tubs.

Corn salad needs a well-drained, rich soil – preferably one manured or composted for a previous crop. Failing this, dig compost into the soil a month or two before sowing and allow it to settle. Choose a sunny, sheltered site; some shade is tolerated. The plants must be kept well watered in dry weather or they will produce poor leaves and run to seed.

Slugs are the main pest and can be controlled with Draza pellets.

Harvest when the plants have produced four or five leaves by gently pulling off one or two from each plant; always leave some for the plant to grow on with.

Recommended varieties 'Large-leaved English'; 'Large-leaved Italian'

Site Open but sheltered
Soil Good, moisture-retentive
Sow Autumn or late-winter to spring
Harvest Autumn to winter and spring to summer, depending on when sown

Courgette *see* Marrow

Corn salad, or lamb's lettuce, is hardier than ordinary lettuce and makes a useful alternative to it in salad dishes. If sown in autumn and then successionally (under cloches) in late winter and spring it will provide a crop for most of the year.

Cress, Land or American

Barbarea verna

Land, or American, cress is actually a European biennial, grown as an annual, that has become naturalised in North America. A low-growing plant, its leaves spread out in a rosette formation and look and taste rather similar to water cress.

Sow successively, a few plants at a time, in small groups or blocks from spring to autumn. They should be spaced, or later thinned, to intervals of 120–150 mm (4½–6 in). The later sowings should be protected by cloches or polythene tunnels; alternatively, the crops may be raised in a cold frame or a grow bag.

Soil should be good and moisture-retentive, with plenty of peat or compost added if necessary. An open site is preferable, but in very warm areas some shade should be provided. Keep the soil well watered in dry weather.

Slugs and snails may be a nuisance and should be dealt with by Draza pellets. Flea beetles should be controlled with derris. If this pest is a particular nuisance in your area, it may be best to sow only in autumn for spring crops.

Harvest when the plants have developed several leaves; pull a few leaves, but not all, from each plant as required.

Site Open; shaded in warm areas
Soil Rich, moisture-retentive
Sow Spring to autumn
Harvest As required when sufficient leaves have developed

Cucumber and Gherkin

Cucumis sativus

Many of the modern outdoor, or ridge, cucumbers grow almost as easily as marrows and so are a welcome addition to a small kitchen garden. They are also longer and less prickly than the older types. They may be grown on the flat (although this takes up a lot of room) or they may be trained up a trellis or (like tomatoes) up a bamboo, or up a wigwam of bamboo sticks. Gherkins are simply smaller-growing varieties of cucumbers. If lack of space is a serious problem and no greenhouse is available, you may grow the greenhouse variety 'Fembaby' indoors in 300 mm (12 in) pots placed by a French window or in some other large, light area.

Sow seeds singly, at a depth of 20–25 mm (¾–1 in), in 75 mm (3 in) pots of proprietary potting compost, in late April to early May in a warm position indoors. Keep the seedlings moist and make sure they do not get scorched in strong sunlight. Harden them off under cloches or in a frame, then plant them out in late May or early June. Seed may alternatively be sown directly in the main plot from mid-May; sow two or three seeds at each point and thin to the strongest

Land cress is an excellent alternative to water cress. It grows readily in moist soil and will often self-sow freely.

Cucumber planting. The site should be warm and sheltered, with direct sunlight. Dig a hole at least 300 mm (12 in) square and deep.

Thoroughly mix the dug soil with about the same amount of compost. Make sure that the mixture is not lumpy, then fill the hole with it.

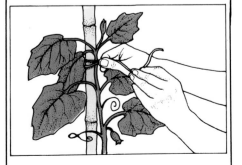

Holding the plant by the root ball, lower it into a hole made in the mixture of soil and compost. Firm it in gently, then water it.

If you train the plant up a support, tie the stem securely at several points – it will later have to bear a considerable weight of fruit.

when the seedlings are established.

The soil must be fairly light and well prepared, with as much compost as you can spare. For each plant dig a hole 300–400 mm (12–15½ in) square and later capped with a 40–50 mm (1½–2 in) mound of soil. The site should be warm and sunny. Young plants will be given a stronger start if protected for a week or two under cloches. In colder areas it may be advisable to grow the cucumbers in frames. Most cucumber plants must be spaced 750–900 mm (30–36 in) apart, but the 'Patio-Pik' variety and gherkins need a space of only about 600 mm (24 in). When about six leaves have grown on each plant, pinch out the growing tip to encourage the development of side shoots; these must then be trained against your supports. Keep the soil well watered and weed-free at all times. Protect plants against slugs and snails with Draza pellets. Any moulds and mildews should be treated with a fungicide such as benomyl or one of the systemics.

Harvest the fruits when young; allowing them to mature fully will spoil their flavour and discourage the plant from producing more fruits. The ridge cucumbers should be 150–200 mm (6–8 in) long and the gherkins should be not more than about 75 mm (3 in).

Recommended varieties 'Burpless Tasty Green', F_1, good under protection; 'Conda', F_1, good-cropping gherkin; 'Crystal Apple', unusual pale-coloured, round cucumber; 'Fembaby', F_1, for pot-growing indoors, short fruit; 'Kyoto', good for training up poles; 'Patio-Pik', may be grown closer, saving space; 'Perfection' ('King of the Ridge'), a popular late-cropper; 'Venlo' ('Venlo Pickling'), a favourite gherkin

Site Sunny, sheltered
Soil Rich and moist, with compost well dug in
Sow Late April–May indoors; late May–June outdoors
Harvest Regularly, before fruits have matured fully

Endive *see* Chicory

Gherkin *see* Cucumber

Kale or Borecole
Brassica oleracea acephala

There are a number of different types of kale, but only two are widely available – curly or Scotch, in tall or dwarf forms, and a hybrid called 'Pentland Brig'. They all produce excellent 'spring greens' and are a useful crop to follow early potatoes.

The sowing and transplanting methods are as for cauliflower. Sow April to May and transplant July to August, spacing the seedlings 500–600 mm (20–24 in) apart. The soil should be rich enough if the crop follows early potatoes, but it may need some high-nitrogen fertiliser around the end of the year.

Pests and diseases: *see* Brassicas.

Harvest from late winter into spring; pick the young leaves of the curly types and young side shoots of 'Pentland Brig' by snapping them off like Brussels sprouts.

Recommended varieties 'Dwarf Green Curled', very curly leaves; 'Pentland Brig', hardy, long-cropping; 'Tall Green Curled', extremely hardy

Site Preferably open
Soil Firm, rich
Sow April to May
Harvest From late winter into spring

Kohlrabi
Brassica oleracea gongylodes

Also known as the turnip cabbage, kohlrabi is a form of cabbage grown for its edible swollen stem, which has a turnip flavour. The stems may be cooked or grated raw for use in salads. Kohlrabi withstands drought better than turnips, so it is a useful crop in warm, dry areas, although the most succulent stems will be produced with plenty of moisture. It is useful as a catch crop.

Sow seed in the main plot in rows or blocks. The growing points should be about 250 mm (10 in) apart for summer and autumn crops, and about 300 mm (12 in) apart if the crop is to be left standing over winter; thin out as necessary. Sowing begins in late March and continues successionally about every four weeks until mid-July. Choose a sunny site. The soil should have plenty of compost incorporated for a previous crop; as with most brassicas, it may need a little lime added. Water the soil in dry weather; keep it weed-free.

Pests and diseases: *see* Brassicas.

Harvest when the swollen part of the stem is about 60 mm (2½ in) in diameter; if allowed to grow longer the stems tend to become strong-flavoured and tough.

Recommended varieties 'Purple Vienna', purple skinned, white flesh; 'White Vienna', pale-green skinned, white flesh

Site Sunny
Soil Rich; may need addition of hydrated lime
Sow March to late summer
Harvest When stems are about 60 mm (2½ in) in diameter

Leaf Beet *see* Beetroot and Leaf beet

RIGHT *The crinkly leaves of 'Dwarf Green Curled' kale make excellent spring greens. Harvest the leaves while they are young.*
BELOW *The swollen stems of kohlrabi are tastiest when no more than 60 mm (2½ in) in diameter. This one is 'White Vienna'.*

Leek

Allium ampeloprasum porrum

Although leeks remain in the ground a long time they are useful plants even for small gardens because they can be spaced fairly closely and crop late. They are hardy plants and easy to grow. The part we value for food is not in fact the stem but a series of tightly wrapped leaves.

Leeks may be grown from seed or from bought plants. Sow 12–20 mm (½–¾ in) deep in a prepared seed bed, and thin out later so that there is room for the seedlings to develop 50–60 mm (2–2½ in) apart. If you use a frame or cloches you can sow in late winter to early spring; if unprotected, sow from early to mid-spring, depending on the weather. Larger sub-

jects transplant better, so the earlier you can sow the better. Transplant when the plants are about 200 mm (8 in) high, in early to mid-summer. The seed bed should be moist when you lift the seedlings.

Transplant (or plant your bought leeks) into holes about 150 mm (6 in) deep made with a dibber; the plants should be 200–250 mm (8–10 in) apart, whether in rows or blocks. Drop each plant into its hole and water it well in – no soil need be added. Some gardeners shorten the leaf tips to prevent them flopping over and rotting or being pulled into the ground by worms.

The soil for leeks should have been well prepared for a previous crop, and with compost dug in after that crop was cleared. Keep the soil weed-free and moist.

Leeks have a tendency to bolt. If the 'stem' is reasonably thick, however, you can snap off the

appendage holding the buds at the end of the flower stem; with luck the leek will remain edible for a while. However if the 'stems' of bolted plants are thin they will be tough and poorly flavoured, and the plants should be dug up and composted.

Harvest when the plants are of a sufficient size, or leave them in the ground until required.

Pests and diseases: *see* Onion and Shallot

Recommended varieties 'Autumn Mammoth' varieties; 'Blue Solaise Medola', blue-green leaves; 'Giant Winter' varieties; 'Lyon-Prizetaker'; 'Musselburgh' varieties

Site Open
Soil Well-composted
Sow Late winter to early spring if protected; early to mid-spring if in the open
Harvest When required

'Webbs Wonderful', one of the most popular of the large cabbage lettuces.

Legumes

Legumes are members of the Leguminosae family. Among vegetables they are represented by various peas and beans, all of which are dwarf or have dwarf forms suitable for smaller gardens. Leguminous plants have nodules on their roots containing bacteria capable of taking up nitrogen from the air. As a consequence, the roots of legumes are a valuable store of nitrogen and should, where possible, be left in the soil when the plants are harvested and cleared from the plot.

Lettuce
Lactuca sativa

Even in the open, lettuce may be grown for a good part of the year; with a little protection, it will grow almost all the year round. It is easy to grow and requires little space. The best method is to sow it successionally, a few seeds at a time, every few weeks, so that you have a more or less continuous supply of succulent leaves. If you have severely restricted space the compact varieties recommended will give you a large number of plants from a small area of plot, or they may be grown in tubs.

A recently introduced method of growing produces a large quantity of leaf at the expense of heart; its advantage is that each plant will produce two crops – which represents another space-saving formula. Experiments have shown that the crisp-leaved cos types are the most suitable for this method. From a sowing in early April and successional ones, first until late May and then from August, leaf crops may be harvested from late May to late October.

Conventional Crops
The following is the method for growing leaf-and-heart lettuce in the normal way. Sow with two or three seeds at each growing point at a depth of 12–20 mm (½–¾ in); thin out to the strongest after germination. The early crops should be sown either in frames or under cloches, the later ones where they are to grow.

The earlies can be transplanted at intervals of 230 mm (9 in) in rows 200 mm (8 in) apart if the plants in alternate rows are staggered; the compact varieties can be packed even closer, at 130 mm (5¼ in) and 110 mm (4½ in) respectively. Later crops should be planted at intervals of 300 mm (12 in), with 270 mm (10½ in) between rows.

Successional sowing at one- or two-week intervals of a few plants at a time will provide a long season of cropping – provided you select the correct varieties (see list below). An alternative is to sow rows or blocks more thickly than recommended above and then thin them out to the required spacings. If the lifted plants have been gently eased out of the soil, with roots intact, they may be replanted, at the normal spacings, in a new row or block, and will mature later than those left undisturbed.

A good well-drained soil enriched with plenty of compost is required. If garden compost is not available use peat mixed with a general fertiliser. A sunny site is best but lettuce may be grown as an early catch crop between rows of later maturing vegetables. Keep watered and weed-free. Overwintering crops will need protection, depending on variety.

The main lettuce pests in a small garden are likely to be leatherjackets, cutworms, slugs, and snails. Aphids may attack overwintering crops, and malathion spray will control these.

Harvest as required, according to variety and sowing date.

Growing for Leaves Only
Certain varieties of the normal cos lettuces respond to close-spaced growing by producing leaves and no hearts; two crops may be obtained from each plant, the first being earlier than that obtained by conventional growing methods. Sow at a depth of 12–20 mm (½–¾ in) at intervals of 20–25 mm (¾–1 in) in rows 130 mm (5 in) apart. The sowing programme is as follows: sow weekly for seven consecutive weeks from the beginning of April and for three consecutive weeks from the beginning of August. Soil, site, and cultivation are as for ordinary growing methods; the August sowings may be on ground cleared of the earlier-sown lettuce.

The earlier sowings can be harvested, from the end of May to the end of August, by cutting the loose heads of leaves off the main stems. These stems, which should be left 20–30 mm (¾–1¼ in) high, will grow the later crops of leaves from this sowing. Treat the August-sown plants in exactly the same way. Crop them, first from the sown plants and then from the regrowth, from early September to late October.

Recommended varieties
LARGE CABBAGE 'All the Year Round', for sowing spring to autumn, slow to bolt; 'Arctic King', for autumn sowing, medium size, very hardy; 'Avoncrisp', for spring and summer sowing, crisp, good quality, resists lettuce mildew and root aphids; 'Avondefiance', for spring and summer sowing, softer-leaved than 'Avoncrisp', resists downy mildew and root aphids; 'Continuity', for spring to summer sowing, reddish tinged outer leaves; 'Hilde' ('Suzan'), for March–July sowing in the open and for January–February sowing under protection for transplanting in March; 'Imperial Winter', for autumn sowing, larger than 'Arctic King'; 'Unrivalled' ('Trocadero Improved'), for spring to autumn sowing in the open and for January–February sowing under protection for transplanting in March; 'Webbs Wonderful', for sowing from early spring onwards, slow to bolt, crisp; 'Winter Density', for spring to autumn sowing, compact, intermediate between cabbage and cos types
LARGE COS (all suitable for hearting or leaf-only production) 'Lobjoits Green Cos', sown in spring onwards for summer crops and in autumn for spring crops, large, crisp; 'Paris White', large, good in hot weather; 'Valmaine', medium large
COMPACT VARIETIES (for growing under cloches or in the open) 'Little Gem' ('Sugar Cos'), for sowing in spring onwards, excellent quality, intermediate between cos and cabbage types; 'Tom Thumb', for spring sowing, fine cabbage type

Site Sunny
Soil Rich, well-drained
Sow Most of the year, depending on varieties
Harvest Most of the year, depending on varieties

Marrow and Squash
Cucurbita species

Many marrows (particularly those used for courgettes) and squashes make compact, bushy plants suitable for small gardens. They can be grown in the main plot or, if space is scarce, in grow bags or tubs (their big leaves and large yellow flowers make quite an interesting feature on a patio). Most squashes have a sweeter, drier-textured flesh (often orange in colour) than marrows and are nearer to the large traditional pumpkins in flavour. They may be boiled whole, cut up and baked, or roasted with a joint of meat. The yellow-skinned 'Golden Zucchini' marrow and the scallop-shaped 'Scallopini' squash can either be cooked in the usual manner or sliced and eaten raw in salads. Squashes need a long period of growth – so sow them early.

The following applies to both marrows and squashes. If started indoors, sow in 75 mm (3 in) peat pots in mid- to late April; if sown outdoors in the main plot, sow two seeds in each growing point at intervals of about 40 mm (1½ in) in mid- to late May, protecting the seeds and seedlings with cloches. Thin later to the strongest seedling at each growing point. Whether grown in pots or outdoors the seeds should be pressed into the growing medium to a depth of 20–25 mm (¾–1 in), covered with soil, and watered in. Gradually harden off the outdoor plants by removing cloches in the mornings on fine days but replacing them at night until danger of frost has passed.

Sunny, sheltered sites are best, and the plants need a rich, moist soil. When the plants have hardened off, prepare them for transplanting as follows. Dig out a hole for each plant about 250 mm (10 in) deep and 350 mm (13½ in) wide and fill with well-rotted compost (or manure if you can get it) and a sprinkling of a general fertiliser. Cover with soil and insert the plants. The sites should be 600–750 mm (24–30 in) apart. Keep the soil well watered.

Pollination is sometimes erratic, especially in cool weather when few pollinating insects are about. Assistance may be given by snapping off an open male flower, stripping it of petals, and pressing the remaining point into the centre of a female flower. It is best to use a new flower for each assisted pollination. Male flowers do not have the swelling behind the flower.

The main pests are slugs and snails and these should be kept under control with slug pellets.

Harvest courgettes when they are 125–150 mm (5–6 in) long; the round marrow 'Tender and True' forms excellent courgettes about 75 mm (3 in) in diameter. Squashes are harvested according to type when ready; 'Scallopini' is about as early as marrows and courgettes, but most squashes are later. Crop regularly to keep plants in production. If left to grow on, most courgettes will form good marrows but the crop will be less numerous. Many squashes and marrows store well in a dry, frost-free place; the zucchini varieties of courgettes are suitable for freezing.

Recommended varieties 'Custard White' and 'Custard Yellow' (marrows), round, yellow or white fruits, best eaten young, semi-bushy; 'Golden Zucchini', F$_1$ (courgette or marrow), yellow fruit, good cropper, bushy; 'Scallopini', F$_1$ (squash), flattish, round, green fruit, sweetish white flesh, best eaten young, semi-bushy; 'Table Ace', F$_1$ (squash), acorn-shaped, dark-green fruits, rich-flavoured yellow flesh, keeps well, semi-bushy; 'Table Queen', F$_1$ (squash), small acorn-shaped fruit, dark-green fruits, rich-flavoured yellow flesh, keeps well, bushy; 'Tender and True' (marrow), suitable for young 'round' courgettes, excellent cropper, semi-bushy; 'Zucchini', F$_1$ ('Early Gem') (courgette or marrow), good cropper, bushy

Site Sunny, sheltered
Soil Rich, moist
Sow Mid- to late April indoors; mid- to late May outdoors under cloches
Harvest From July onwards according to variety and usage

LEFT *Male and female marrow flowers (top). Male flower stripped (centre) for assisted pollination of the female. Some typical marrows and squashes (bottom, left to right): marrow, yellow zucchinis, 'Custard White', 'Golden Zucchini', 'Table Queen'.*

RIGHT *A popular marrow, 'Tender and True'.*

Onion and Shallot
Allium species

Although there are many different types of onion, not all lend themselves to cultivation in the small garden. Red varieties of the common onion are rarely on sale in shops but are most attractive in dishes requiring raw onion. Two types of onion and the closely related shallot will fulfil most of the usual onion needs.

The common bulbous onion, *Allium cepa*, is grown from 'sets' (small bulbs) or seed sown in spring; to extend the cropping season you can also use the autumn-sown Japanese varieties. The shallot, a variety of *A. cepa aggregatum*, is prolific and a true all-rounder; although small the bulbs may be used in cooking in the same way as the larger common onions, or they may be used as spring onions or for pickling. These two types may be supplemented by growing another species specifically for salads. A good choice would be the Japanese bunching onion, *A. fistulosum*, also known as onion leeks.

Common Onion
Sow thinly at a depth of 12–20 mm (½–¾ in) in rows 300 mm (12 in) apart from mid-April or from early to mid-autumn depending on variety. Thin the spring-sown onions gradually until the remaining plants are 40–150 mm (1½–6 in) apart. Thin autumn-sown varieties in the spring, using the lifted ones as spring onions.

Sown onions require soil well enriched with compost dug in a month or two previously and allowed to settle. A sunny site is preferable.

In damper and colder areas, and if raising plants from seed proves difficult, use onion sets instead of seed. Ask for heat-treated sets if you are buying them. The sets are planted in the main plot on ground that was well composted for a previous crop. Space the sets 50–150 mm (2–6 in) apart in rows 250 mm (10 in) apart or in blocks. Cover the sets lightly with soil, firm them in, and water. To prevent the plants from bolting the soil should be moist (but not too wet) at all times. Keep the soil free of weeds.

When the crop is approaching maturity, bend the tops over just above the bulbs to allow the maximum sunshine for ripening. The leaves will gradually yellow and dry, and the bulbs should then be gently lifted with a fork and laid on the surface to dry out. (In a wet season however, it may be necessary to dry them off under cover on racks of wire netting.)

On dry soils the commonest pest is the onion fly. The bulbs are attacked by the fly maggots and become mushy and rot; if this happens dig up the affected bulbs and burn them. The pest will be deterred to some extent if you sprinkle calomel dust into the soil when sowing or planting, and by spraying the plants with one of the trichlorphon insecticides every few weeks during growth.

Unless you are using the onions immediately after lifting, those harvested in autumn can be hung in 'ropes' or nets in a dry, frost-free place. The autumn-sown, summer-lifted types are not good keepers and should be used as soon as possible after harvesting.

Recommended varieties
SEED (spring-sown for autumn harvesting) 'Ailsa Craig', popular, large (use maximum spacing); 'Bedfordshire Champion', good keeper; 'Brunswick' ('Blood Red'), red variety, good keeper; 'Hygro', F_1, excellent keeper; 'Rijnsburger' selections; 'Southport Red Globe', attractive red variety
SEED (autumn-sown for summer harvesting) 'Express Yellow O-X'; 'Imai Early Yellow'; 'Senshyu Semi-Globe Yellow'
SETS (spring-sown for autumn harvesting) 'Brunswick' ('Blood Red'); 'Giant Fen Globe'; 'Rijnsburger-Wijbo'; 'Sturon'; 'Stuttgart Giant'

Shallot
Plant as for onion sets, at intervals of 150 mm (6 in) in rows 100 mm (4 in) apart. Harvest as 'spring onions' when required, either by gently breaking individuals off the growing clumps or by lifting whole clumps. Mature bulb clumps are lifted, sep-

These wide-spaced rows of shallots are being grown with a catch-crop of lettuce. Inset: Japanese onions.

arated, dried, and stored as for onions; they are good keepers.

Most seedsmen sell reliable varieties with either yellowish brown or reddish brown skins.

Japanese Bunching Onion

These provide, if sown successionally, an almost continuous supply of long spring onions. Sow in soil and site similar to those for common onions, or as an intercrop. August sowings provide spring crops; late-winter and early-summer sowings are harvested, respectively, in summer and autumn. Sow to a depth of 6 mm (¼ in) in rows 200–250 mm (8–10 in) apart. Harvest as required seven to nine weeks after sowing, or longer in poor weather.

Recommended varieties 'Hikari'; 'Ishikuro'; 'Kincho'; 'Long White Tokyo'

Site Sunny
Soil Good
Sow Spring or autumn according to variety; plant sets in spring
Harvest As required according to variety

Parsnip
Pastinaca sativa

Parsnips in general have a long growing season, and a sizeable crop occupies a lot of space – neither of which features offers encouragement to owners of small kitchen gardens. But, if you are fond of these useful plants, the excellent small 'Avonresister' needs far less space than other varieties and could make a welcome addition to your vegetables.

Sow from March in the north and in April or May in the south. Sow two or three seeds at each growing point at a depth of 12–20 mm (½–¾ in). Allow 75 mm (3 in) between growing points and 200 mm (8 in) between rows. Thin the seedlings to intervals of one every 75 mm (3 in).

Parsnips need soil that was well composted for a previous crop. Dig the soil thoroughly in the autumn and break it down to a smoother surface only when preparing to sow. Shortly before sowing sprinkle and

rake in a general fertiliser. The site should be moist and not too shady, and must be kept free of weeds.

Harvest from autumn onwards; the flavour is reckoned to improve after frost. The plants may be left in the ground until required. Any remaining the following March should be lifted and stored in boxes of sand or soil to prevent re-growth.

Canker is a frequent source of trouble with parsnips, but 'Avonresister' shows good resistance to it.

Recommended variety 'Avonresister'

Site Most, not too shady
Soil Well prepared for a previous crop; moist
Sow Spring
Harvest Autumn onwards

Peas
Pisum sativum varieties

Since you can buy reasonably priced frozen peas of good quality it might seem pointless to grow this vegetable in a small kitchen garden. The justification – if you need one – is that some of the modern dwarf varieties take up little space, and that some of the rarer varieties are seldom available in many shops. Good examples of the latter are the mangetout ('eat-all') varieties, or sugar peas, and the newer snap peas. The latter are allowed to thicken up rather like a French bean; they can be eaten pod and all when young, and later like French beans or with the pods and peas served separately. Of the two main groups of peas, the round-seeded varieties are nowadays used mainly for winter and early spring sowing. Most of the varieties recommended here, however, belong to the wrinkle-seeded group, which have a superior flavour to the round-seeded types.

First early sowings are made in early March and second earlies from mid-April to May; maincrop sowings of ordinary varieties are in May–June. Sugar pea varieties are sown in mid-April to May. Sow the seeds in a flat-bottomed drill (that is, a continuous furrow rather than individual holes). The drill should be 40 mm (1½ in) deep and 150 mm (6

in) wide. The seeds can be sown zig-zag fashion in the drill and spaced 120 mm (4½ in) apart. If you sow more than one drill the space between drills should equal the height to which the variety in question will grow (see list below). Cloches will encourage earlier growth as well as protect the plants against cold weather and bird damage.

Peas thrive in a sunny site and a rich, moisture-retentive soil. If the soil was not well composted for a previous crop, add plenty of compost and allow to settle for a while; sprinkle on a general fertiliser before sowing. Keep the soil moist and weed free. Supports such as pea netting between stakes will be essential for the taller varieties.

Of many pests and diseases that may attack peas, the commonest source of trouble is the caterpillar of the pea moth, especially on the maincrops. The maggot-like caterpillar bores through the pods and into the peas. Spray the plants 10 days or so after they flower (June to mid-August) with a gamma-HCH (BHC) or fenitrothion insecticide; this will also help to control attacks of aphids and thrips.

Harvest green peas as they become ready. The difference between varieties described as 'first early', 'maincrop', and so on is in the time each requires between sowing and harvesting; first earlies are the quickest-growing. Sugar peas are harvested before the peas begin to swell the pods; 'Sugar Snap', however, may be cropped then or allowed to mature like an ordinary variety.

Recommended varieties Figures given are the approximate heights of the mature plants
ORDINARY PEAS (all wrinkle-seeded) 'Early Onward' (early maincrop), may be sown successionally, good for freezing, 600–750 mm (24–30 in); 'Hurst Beagle' (first early), 450–500 mm (18–20 in); 'Hurst Green Shaft' (maincrop), heavy cropper, sweet, good for freezing, 600–750 mm (24–30 in); 'Kelvedon Wonder' (first early), may be sown successionally, heavy

Maincrop green pea 'Hurst Green Shaft', a high-quality, heavy-cropping variety that is also suitable for freezing.

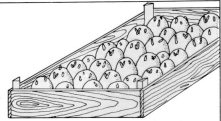

Seed potatoes are chitted (made to sprout) before planting by storing them, closely packed with 'eye' ends upward, from autumn until spring.

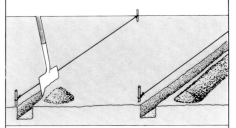

Trenches for maincrop tubers should be 150 mm (6 in) wide and deep and 750 mm (30 in) apart. The soil should have been enriched with compost.

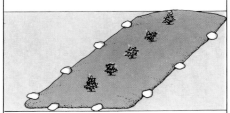

Black polythene sheet is placed, with edges anchored, over each row. The plants emerge through slits in sheet.

As an alternative to plastic sheet, earth up the shoots, raising the height of the ridge as the plants grow. Keep ridge moist.

cropper, good for freezing, 450–500 mm (18–20 in); 'Little Marvel' (early), may be sown successionally, good under cloches, 400–500 mm (16–20 in); 'Onward' (maincrop), good cropper, good for freezing, 600–800 mm (24–32 in); 'Progress No. 9' (first early), may be sown successionally, 450–600 mm (18–24 in)

SUGAR OR MANGETOUT PEAS 'Dwarf Sweet Green', 600–900 mm (24–36 in); 'Sugar Snap', 1·2–1·5 m (4–5 ft); 'Tezieravenir, average 800 mm (32 in)

Site Sunny
Soil Rich, moist
Sow Early spring to early summer
Harvest According to variety

Perpetual spinach *see* Beetroot and Leaf Beat

Potato
Solanum tuberosum

Potatoes are hardly worth growing in a small garden unless one concentrates on early varieties to provide 'new' potatoes or on good-quality unusual varieties that are rarely available in the shops. Of the unusual varieties only 'Pink Fir Apple' seems to be offered from time to time. Its pink-skinned tubers are often strangely shaped, but they retain their quality as 'new' potatoes well into the winter, when 'new' varieties in the shops are either very expensive or unobtainable. It is excellent when eaten hot and buttered or cold with salads. As it is a maincrop variety, it needs more space to grow than the earlies.

Potatoes are grown from selected small tubers known as 'seed' potatoes; make sure you buy only those certified as virus-free. The tubers must then be 'chitted' – that is, allowed to sprout from 'eyes' at the end opposite the point of attachment to the parent plant – before they are sown. For this purpose place your seed potatoes close together and with 'eye' ends upwards, in tomato boxes, seed or egg trays, or other suitable containers. Early varieties of seed potatoes should be bought in the autumn and kept at a temperature of about 18°C (66°F) until one or two

sprouts have just started to develop on each tuber; then they should be stored at about 7°C (40°F) until the spring. Finally, about a week before planting, put them in a warm, light place so that they will produce good sprouts. Alternatively, store the earlies at 7–10°C (40–50°F), then rub out all but two or three sprouts on each tuber before planting. Maincrop seed potatoes should also be stored at 7–10°C (40–50°F) until planting time; do *not* rub off any of the sprouts on these later varieties.

The soil must have been well dug the previous autumn, with plenty of compost thoroughly mixed in. The site should if possible be sheltered to minimise the effects of frost. The earlies are planted in March and the maincrop at the end of April. Take out a trench about 150 mm (6 in) wide and deep. Plant the earlies 300 mm (12 in) apart, and the maincrop 400 mm (16 in) apart. If you plant more than one row the trenches should be 600 mm (24 in) apart for the earlies and 750 mm (30 in) for the maincrop. After covering the tubers with soil, rake in a general fertiliser.

Two alternative methods may now be used to grow the crop: covering the soil with black polythene sheet, or earthing up. In the first, the polythene sheet over each row of earlies must be at least 600 mm (24 in) wide and over each maincrop row at least 750 mm (30 in). Bury the edges of the sheet at sides and ends with soil weighted with heavy stones. When the sprouts emerge from the soil after a few weeks, cut a slit in the sheet immediately above each so that the plants can grow through. Too much light will cause the development of green and possibly poisonous tubers, so heap peat around the slits and plant stems.

To earth up your potatoes draw up soil from between the rows with a hoe or rake when the plant shoots are 150–200 mm (6–8 in) tall. The idea is to build up a ridge along the row, leaving the top 75–90 mm (3–3½ in) of each shoot exposed. Raise the height of the ridge every week or 10 days, always ensuring that about half the total height of the stem remains above the top until the ridge is about 150 mm (6 in) high. Keep the ridge moist: it tends to dry out quicker than the surrounding soil.

If you have no space to grow even early potatoes in the main plot, you can raise some in large pots, plastic buckets, or tubs (if using buckets, however, you must drill drainage holes in the bottom). A bucket-sized container will take two seed potatoes; the largest will take up to 9 or 10. The growing medium should be a John Innes or soil-less compost, or well-broken-down garden soil enriched with garden compost and with a sprinkling of general fertiliser. Plant the seed potatoes in March. Keep the soil moist but not wet; shelter or cover the containers in very rainy weather, but uncover them again as soon as possible. Protect the plants against night frost by covering the containers with old sacks, curtains, or anything else suitable. Earth up the plants with John Innes No. 3 or an equivalent soil-less compost.

Harvesting of new potatoes usually begins in June. For the earliest ones of all, remove a little soil carefully from around the plants (or lift the polythene), select the largest potatoes, and re-cover the remainder to grow on and be cropped in a similar fashion. Later, in July, the plants may be lifted by carefully forking them up – but be careful not to damage the tubers with the tines of the fork. Potatoes not required for immediate use should be dried and stored. Maincrop 'Pink Fir Apple' will be ready in the autumn when the foliage dies down. Lift them as above, dry them well, and store them in the dark in boxes in a cool but frost-free place. Earlies grown in containers will be ready slightly before those in the main plot – probably from late May. After you have harvested all the tubers, the compost and containers can be used for growing radishes, carrots, or lettuce.

The commonest potato pest is wireworm, which bores holes into the tubers; it is especially likely to cause trouble on newly cultivated ground. Bromophos will give some control. Eelworm, another nuisance, does not usually cause trouble if your crops are correctly rotated. Two fungal diseases, scab and blight, may also occur. Scab forms raised patches and spots on the tubers but does not otherwise affect their quality. It is commonest in alkaline soils, for which scab-resistant varieties are available. Blight, on the other hand, can ruin your crop. The visible signs are on the leaves which develop brownish yellow patches in dry weather and shrivel, or become covered on the undersides with white threads in wetter conditions. Blight attacks the tubers, their skins developing greyish patches and the flesh reddish brown. All the affected tubers, stems, and leaves should be lifted and burnt as soon as the symptoms appear. Fungicides such as Bordeaux mixture, maneb, or zineb will help to prevent blight.

Recommended varieties
FIRST EARLY 'Arran Pilot', best in the south, resists scab; 'Foremost', good in Scotland, susceptible to scab; 'Home Guard', an old favourite; 'Maris Bard', a newer variety, earlier than 'Pentland Javelin'; 'Pentland Javelin', resists some eelworms
MAINCROP 'Pink Fir Apple', retains 'new' potato quality well and is good in salads

Site Sheltered
Soil Richly organic, not limy
Plant Earlies February to March; maincrop April to May
Harvest Earlies, June to July; maincrop, autumn; store in dark, cool but frost-free place

Radish
Raphanus sativus

There are many varieties of radish, but only a few offer any special advantages over the others in terms of flavour, while some are unsatisfactory in confined areas owing to the length of their roots. The four varieties recommended are suitable for small gardens. Salad radishes are excellent as intercrops or for growing in odd unoccupied areas; they must be kept moist and growing quickly to prevent them becoming tough and hot flavoured. The earliest salad radishes need the protection of a frame or cloche. Successional sowing, every 10 days or so, of a few seeds at a time from spring into late summer will give a long season of cropping. Besides the typical salad radishes there are also the winter varieties, which are much larger rooted and are sown in late summer. They may be sliced and eaten raw or cooked in stews.

With salad radishes the earliest sowings are made under cloches or in frames from early February; unprotected sowings begin about mid-

The early radish variety 'French Breakfast Forcing' makes a good start to the season.

March, preferably on sheltered sites. Radish seeds are large enough to sow individually. Salad radish seeds should be sown 25 mm (1 in) apart and 20–25 mm (¾–1 in) deep, with 100–150 mm (4–6 in) space between rows. Winter radishes are sown about 150 mm (6 in) apart with 180 mm (7 in) between rows, from mid-July in the north of England and from August in the south. Water in.

Sites should be warm and sheltered for early sowings but shady for later ones. The soil must be rich, preferably having been well composted for a previous crop. Keep it moist in dry weather, but do not overwater the plants.

The main pests are slugs and snails, which can be controlled by pellets. Flea beetles may make small holes in the leaves.

Harvest the early radishes when suitably sized, from about early April. 'Red Prince', recommended for maincrop salad sowings, will grow to a large size without loss of quality. Take a first harvest of this variety by removing alternate radishes in each row, allowing the remainder to grow on until needed. The winter radish may be harvested as soon as it is large enough.

Recommended varieties
EARLIES 'French Breakfast Forcing'; 'Saxerre'
MAINCROP 'Red Prince'
WINTER 'Black Spanish Round'

Site Early crops, sheltered and warm; later crops, shady
Soil Rich
Sow Protected, early February; unprotected, from mid-March; winter, mid-July to August
Harvest As required

Salsify and Scorzonera
Tragopogon porrifolius and *Scorzonera hispanica*

These plants are grown mainly for their edible roots. They are dealt with together because they belong to the same family, are grown in much the same ways, and are somewhat similar in taste. Salsify roots have whitish skins, scorzonera blackish brown. For the table they may be fried in butter or boiled. Some growers do not harvest the roots but allow the plants to grow into a second season and harvest the young shoots, which can be blanched and eaten raw in salads or cooked and eaten as asparagus. This is not recommended for small gardens, however.

Sow salsify in April or May and scorzonera in May. The seeds should be sown at a depth of 12–20 mm (½–¾ in), with two or three seeds per growing point, and at intervals of 250 mm (10 in) between points. When the seedlings emerge, thin to the strongest at each point. As the mature roots are very long, on heavy soils it is advisable to prepare the holes at the growing points with a crowbar to a depth of about 300 mm (12 in) or more, and then to fill the holes with potting compost.

The soil should be light, well-drained, and well-composted for a previous crop; do *not* use fresh garden compost or the plants may develop forked roots. Keep the soil weed-free and moist.

Harvest from October onwards.

Recommended varieties
SALSIFY 'Sandwich Island'
SCORZONERA 'Giant Russian'

Site Not too shady
Soil Light, rich, well-drained
Sow April–May
Harvest October onwards

Savoy *see* Cabbage

Shallot *see* Onion

Spinach
Spinacia oleracea varieties and *Tetragonia tetragonoides*

In catalogues the *S. oleracea* varieties are often listed as round-seeded (summer) and prickly seeded (winter) spinach; the seasons refer to their times of harvesting, although the round-seeded form will in fact also grow in winter. New Zealand spinach, *T. tetragonoides*, is a much larger plant, producing triangular leaves, and crops from late summer onwards; it is useful because it grows well in hot, dry weather and on poorer soils that are adequately moist. Round-seeded spinach is successionally sown at fortnightly intervals from March into early summer; prickly seeded is sown successively from July to late September; New Zealand is sown in May–June (or, in pots, in March and then hardened off for planting out in June). Sow two or three seeds at each growing point at a depth of 12–20 mm (½–¾ in), and thin later. The round- and prickly seeded growing points should be 200 mm (8 in) apart, the New Zealand 500 mm (20 in) apart, staggered in either rows or blocks. Early crops can be obtained if you halve these spacings, taking alternate plants when they are young and leaving the rest to grow on. New Zealand seeds are hard and you will aid their germination by soaking them in water overnight before sowing.

Early sowings need an open but sheltered site; later sowings will benefit from partial shading by other crops to prevent bolting; New Zealand will grow in a hotter, sunny site. The round-seeded varieties need deep, rich, moisture-retentive soils; prickly seeded need rich, well-drained soils; New Zealand need light, well-drained soils.

Harvest when the leaves are large enough. Remove only two or three leaves at a time from each plant from round- and prickly seeded; New Zealand may be more heavily cut.

Recommended varieties
ROUND-SEEDED 'Clearleaf', a 'Viking' selection; 'Dominant'; 'Longstanding Round'; 'Noorman' ('Miragreen'); 'Supergreen'
PRICKLY SEEDED 'Broad Leaved Prickly' ('Giant Prickly')
NEW ZEALAND No varieties

Site Open early, shaded later
Soil Deep, rich for prickly and round-seeded; light for New Zealand
Sow Round-seeded, March to early summer; prickly seeded, July to late September; New Zealand, May to June
Harvest When ready

Squash *see* Marrow

Salsify (left) and scorzonera – two tasty roots that can be fried or boiled.

Swede
Brassica napus napobrassica

The swede, also known as rutabaga, is most popular in the north of England, and indeed is easier to grow in the cooler, wetter areas of the country. Like other brassicas it takes up quite a lot of space in the garden, so if you have only a small plot you will need to plan your cropping programme carefully if you intend to grow cabbages, sprouts, broccoli, or cauliflower as well.

Sow in May in the north and in mid-June in the south; water the rows before sowing to help germination. Sow at a depth of 20–25 mm (¾–1 in), with two or three seeds at each growing point and with 400 mm (16 in) between each point. If you stagger the positions of the growing points in alternate rows, the rows can be spaced only 200 mm (8 in) apart. Thin to the strongest seedlings at each point. The soil should have been dug well in the autumn or winter, with compost thoroughly mixed in for a previous crop. Like all brassicas swedes will not tolerate acid soils. Before sowing break the soil down to remove any lumps, and work in a general fertiliser and also hydrated lime if necessary (*see* Brassicas for quantities of lime required). Keep the soil moist.

Pests and diseases: *see* Brassicas.

Harvest as required in late autumn and winter in milder areas. In cold areas it may be best to store the mature roots. Lift the plants, remove their tops, and place the roots in boxes of sand in a cool, frost-free place; alternatively, they may be stored in clamps, where they will keep better than turnips.

Recommended varieties 'Marian'; 'Sutton's Western Perfection' (both these varieties resist club root)

Site Most
Soil Good, moist, and enriched with compost; add lime if necessary
Sow May in the north, mid-June in the south
Harvest Late autumn and winter

'Sutton's Western Perfection' is one of the newer varieties of swede, with good resistance to club-root disease.

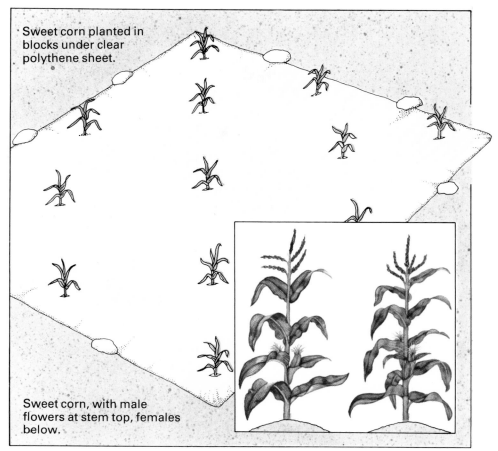

Sweet corn planted in blocks under clear polythene sheet.

Sweet corn, with male flowers at stem top, females below.

Sweet Corn
Zea mays

To be at its best sweet or sugar corn needs a warm soil to start in and warm weather to grow and ripen in: if you live in a cold northern area it is unlikely that the plants will thrive. Only varieties specially bred for gardens should be used; some of the best are listed below. The plants at maturity may be anything from 1·5 to 3 m (5–10 ft) high, and this should be taken into account when planning your cropping programme as they may cast shade over neighbouring crops. The plants will grow better if you warm the soil several weeks before sowing. You can do this by laying clear polythene 25–50-gauge sheet over the area to be planted. Sow the seeds through holes punched in the sheet: the seedlings will then emerge through the holes. If you use this method of mulching, bury the edges of the polythene sheet and anchor them with stones.

Sow two seeds 20–40 mm (¾–1½ in) deep at each growing point in late April to mid-May in the south and in late May in warmer northern areas. Alternatively, you can sow indoors – two seeds per 75 mm (3 in) pot – about three weeks earlier in each case, then transplant at the dates indicated. In the garden the plants should be in blocks rather than long rows in order to help pollination. The plants should be spaced 250 mm (10 in) apart, with 400 mm (16 in) between the block rows, with the growing points staggered in alternate rows; this gives an effective 350 mm (14 in) between each plant and its neighbours in all directions. Thin to the stronger plant at each point. As the plants grow, give them extra support by drawing up soil around the base of the stem.

The site should be sunny and protected against winds. The soil should be neither very light nor heavy; it must drain well, and it should have been thoroughly dug in the winter, with compost incorporated for a previous crop. Add a scattering of general fertiliser before sowing. Keep the soil moist in dry weather, especially after the plants flower. Pinch out any side shoots that appear.

Unless the weather is exception-

ally warm and the plants very vigorous, do not allow more than three or perhaps four cobs to grow on each plant. When the male tassels at the top of the plant are ready they shed pollen onto the female flowers below. You can help this shedding process by tapping the stems of the plants. Eventually the green sheath covering each cob swells as the fruit inside develops. Test for ripeness by peeling away a small piece of the sheath and pressing two or three of the grains with the edge of your thumb nail. If the grain is ripe, a milky juice will spurt out. If the juice is clear and watery, the corn is not yet ripe; if it is very thick or doughy it is over-ripe and will be tough.

Harvest the cobs when they are ready. They should be cooked and eaten as soon as possible as they will dry out quickly.

Recommended varieties All the following are early, and so have a better chance of ripening in our climate; all are sweet, some slightly more so than others: 'Aztec', F_1; 'Earliglo'; 'Extra Early Sweet', F_1; 'Kelvedon Kandy Cob', F_1; 'Kelvedon Sweetheart', F_1

Site Sunny, sheltered
Soil Good, well-drained
Sow April to mid-May in south; late May in north
Harvest Autumn

Tomato
Lycopersicon lycopersicum

The advent of grow bags has made a great contribution to easy tomato growing, and allows the owner of a small garden to make full use of the main plot for other crops. Another great advance of recent years is the improvement of bush tomato varieties, which need neither staking nor pinching out. Some of these varieties, moreover, are superior in flavour to greenhouse-grown ones. Tomatoes can also be grown in window boxes and large pots, and some varieties are even recommended for

Sweet corn plants pollinate themselves more readily if they are planted in blocks rather than rows. Inset: ripe cobs of 'Kelvedon Sweetheart'.

hanging baskets. There is, however, no escaping the fact that your tomatoes will be juicy and fine-flavoured only if they have sufficient heat. It is pointless trying to raise good-quality tomatoes outdoors in cold areas – or even in normally warm southern areas if the summer is colder than usual. The great advantage of grow bags or other containers for tomatoes grown outdoors is that they can be placed against a south-facing, or preferably south-west-facing, wall, which is invariably the warmest place in the garden and receives the most sunlight.

Sow the seeds indoors in a box or in peat pots containing John Innes No 1 compost. The seeds should be sown at a depth of 20–25 mm ($\frac{3}{4}$–1 in). Use only one seed in small peat pots; in boxes the seeds should be 75 mm (3 in) apart. The compost must be kept moist. Put the box and/or pots in a polythene bag and place in a warm, light position. The temperature should be not less than 16°C (63°F) and not more than 25°C (75°F). When the seedlings appear, remove the polythene bag.

Harden off by placing the seedlings outdoors in a sunny, sheltered site under cloches or in a frame; after a week or two, removing the covering on warmer days at first, then continuously until they are completely unprotected. They will then be ready to plant into their growing sites. Stronger plants will be obtained if each of the boxed seedlings is carefully transferred into an individual pot containing John Innes No 2 and allowed to grow on before beginning the hardening off. Before transplanting tomato plants keep watering to the minimum, but do not allow the compost to dry out.

If the tomatoes are grown in the main plot it must be sheltered and have plenty of direct sunlight throughout the day. The soil should have been well enriched with plenty of compost dug in in the previous autumn. Space staking plants 400 mm (16 in) apart and bush plants 480 mm (19 in) apart; this close spacing helps the crop to ripen earlier. In tubs, window boxes, and grow bags use John Innes No 3, spacing the plants as above; the growing medium should be kept moist. Unless the weather is very dry, tomatoes grow-

ing in the main plot will need little watering until the fruit is setting, when plenty should be given.

For tomatoes which need staking, make sure the plants are tied regularly, every 150–200 mm (6–8 in) or so, to keep them firm: they will carry a considerable weight when the trusses of fruit are setting. Bush plants will tend to sag when the trusses are setting; keep the fruits clean by putting straw under the plants. On staked plants, pinch out the side shoots which develop at the angle made between the main stem and leaf stalk. When the first fruit truss has set, cut off the top of the main stem above a leaf to leave 4 or 5 trusses in various stages of development. Do *not* pinch out side shoots from bush-type tomato plants.

Keep the soil weed-free. Feed the plants with diluted liquid fertiliser formulated for tomatoes at every watering or according to the manufacturers' instructions.

Regular spraying with water when the trusses are in flower, followed by a tap on the canes or plant stems, will assist pollination.

Avoid growing tomatoes in soil used in the last two or three years for potatoes; tomato plants will become stunted if attacked by potato-cyst eelworm. The commonest disease to affect outdoor tomatoes is blight, which causes the leaves to develop brownish grey edges and the fruits areas of brownish marbling. Treat blight with a copper, maneb, or zineb fungicide.

Harvest the tomatoes when ripe. Late in the season, ripening may be hastened if you can protect plants with cloches or other transparent cover; alternatively, remove the trusses and store them indoors in a warm place out of direct sunlight.

Recommended varieties
BUSH 'Alfresco', F_1, compact, good crops of good flavour, grows 380–450 mm (15–18 in) high; 'Pixie', F_1, abundant fruits of good flavour; 'Roma', long, oval-fruited continental type; 'Tiny Tim', small fruits of good flavour, suitable for pots and window boxes, grows about 380 mm (15 in) high

'Roma', one of the oval-fruited continental varieties of bush tomato.

STAKING 'Ailsa Craig', well-flavoured; 'Alicante', good flavour and good cropper; 'Gardener's Delight', small, sweet-flavoured fruit; 'Golden Sunrise', excellent-flavoured, yellow fruit; 'Outdoor Girl', early fruiting; 'Sweet 100', F₁, small sweet fruits in abundance, fairly early

Site Sunny, sheltered
Soil Main plot, enriched with compost; containers, John Innes No 3
Sow March to April
Harvest From end of July

Turnip
Brassica rapa

Unless you live in an area which is always cool and moist, summer turnip crops are not easy to grow successfully; extra watering is apt to reduce the flavour. Turnips are not as hardy as swedes but otherwise require the same cultural conditions. Follow the growing instructions for swedes (page 61), but note the different timings and spacings given below. Turnips may, incidentally, be grown to provide some spring greens.

For roots, sow in frames or under cloches in February for early crops. If unprotected, sow first from late March to April, then from late July to August (the last sowings will provide roots for storage). Sow at a depth of 20–25 mm (¾–1 in), with two or three seeds at each growing point. Stagger the growing points in alternate rows: the points should be 250 mm (10 in) apart, with 130 mm (5¼ in) between rows. Thin to the best seedling at each point. For further cultivation, pests and diseases, *see* Swede. For spring greens, sow thinly 20–25 mm (¾–1 in) deep in rows 250 mm (10 in) apart in late August.

Harvest the roots of early turnips when they are golf- to tennis-ball size. Later crops should be lifted in October–November for storing; twist the tops off, and place the roots in boxes of dry sand in a dry, cool, but frost-free place.

Recommended varieties
EARLY-SOWN 'Marteau' ('Jersey Navet'), long-rooted, white, very early, suitable for sowing under protection; 'Milan Purple Top Forcing' ('Sprinter'), flat-rooted, very early, suitable for sowing under protection; 'Milan White', flat, early, white; 'Purple Top Milan', flat, early, purple and white; 'Snowball' ('Early White Stone', 'Model White', 'Six Weeks'), globe-rooted, white; 'Tokyo Cross', F₁, globe-rooted, white
LATE-SOWN 'Golden Ball' ('Orange Jelly'), globe-rooted, yellow skin and flesh, the best for overwintering; 'Manchester Market' ('Green Top Stone'), globe-rooted, half green, half white; 'Purple Top White Globe', globe-rooted, red-topped
SPRING GREENS 'Imperial Green Globe' ('Green Globe', 'Green-top White'), also suitable for late sowing for roots

Site Most
Soil Good, limy, moist
Sow From February under protection; in open, late March to April and late July to August
Harvest Early-sown when 50–75 mm (2–3 in) in diameter, May–June; later sowings in late October–November for storing

'Purple Top Milan', a good early turnip.

Herbs

Almost without exception, fresh herbs are superior to bought herbs because the latter will have been cropped days, weeks, or months before they are sold and will have lost some of their flavour and scent; indeed, many fresh herbs are not marketable at all because they wilt too quickly. Although several hundred species of herbs are available in Britain, only a small proportion of these are in general use in our kitchens. Most herbs are easy to grow (some, indeed, spread and seed perhaps too easily); and although most need warmth and as sheltered a site as possible, they will often thrive in poorer soils than vegetable crops. The following are 22 of the most popular herbs used in Britain.

Balm
Melissa officinalis

Balm, also known as lemon balm from its aromatic leaves, is an easily grown perennial and an excellent flavouring substitute for lemon peel. One or two plants will suffice for most families; in fact, unless you are careful, self-sown seedlings may quickly become a nuisance, so the plant should best be grown in an out-of-the-way spot. The mature plant is 300–600 mm (12–24 in) high.

Sow one or two seeds from April to June. Minimum preparation is required but, to get the plants off to a good start, heavy soil should be lightened. Alternatively, sow a few seeds in a half pot or small box, indoors or out, and transplant the seedlings when they have developed a few leaves. Keep the soil weed-free and watered until the plants are well established. Harvest the leaves when bushy clumps have developed. Clumps may become large and need dividing after a year or two.

Site Almost anywhere except in deep shade
Soil Almost any; very heavy soils should be lightened
Sow Spring to summer
Harvest When required

Lemon balm is one of the easiest herbs to grow. Good with fish and stews, it also makes an excellent companion for parsley sauce.

Basil, Sweet
Ocimum basilicum

Sweet basil is a fragrantly aromatic herb. Used in small quantities its leaves add flavour to salads, veal, curries, and Italian dishes. It is a half-hardy annual and so has to be raised every year: three or four plants should be sufficient for your annual needs. Unlike many herbs, basil repays care in cultivation.

Sow two or three seeds in a small box or a half pot, or single seeds in small pots, in March, and repeat successionally. Raise the seedlings on an indoor window sill, or in a greenhouse, at a temperature above 13°C (56°F). Prick out the seedlings from boxes or half pots and pot them up individually; then harden them off, under a cloche or frame, before planting them out in June (do not transplant earlier than this because the seedlings will be killed by the slightest frost). They should be spaced about 250 mm (10 in) apart. The soil should be prepared with organic material such as compost thoroughly dug in, and the site should be sunny. Alternatively, pot on into larger pots containing John Innes No 2 or 3 or Levington compost. Keep the soil or compost watered in dry weather. Pinch out the flower spikes as they appear to induce bushier growth.

Harvest the leaves as required. They may be preserved by drying, freezing, or keeping in jars of olive oil. For this last method, which preserves the flavour best, clean and dry fresh leaves, put them in the jar, sprinkling salt over the layers as you go, and finally cover the contents with olive oil. Seal the jar.

Varieties In Britain only the type plant is normally sold for culinary use, but some firms supply a purple-leaved form for ornamental purposes which also has the typical flavour.

Site Sunny
Soil Good, well drained, enriched with compost
Sow March onwards, successionally, indoors in pots
Transplant June
Harvest As required; preserve for winter use

Bay
Laurus nobilis

Bay, whose leaves add flavour to casseroles, is a really versatile evergreen shrub or tree that will grow in the confined space of a small tub as well as in the open except in cold, wet areas. As it may develop into a large bush, take care where you site your plant, or be prepared to keep it trimmed. It is attractive enough to grow in a bed or border or, potted, on a patio, and it provides interest and value throughout the year. Tub-grown plants may be trimmed to form decorative shapes.

Plant in the spring in a well-dug site in the garden or into John Innes or Levington composts if it is to be tub-grown. In the garden, most soils except heavy waterlogged ones are suitable, but the site should be sunny. If grown in the garden, keep the soil moist until the plant is established; tub-grown plants will need regular watering.

Pests and diseases are rarely a major problem. Scale insects may become troublesome as they exude a sticky liquid. They can be kept at bay with a systemic insecticide such as dimethoate or malathion. Take care to observe the necessary interval between spraying and using the leaves for cooking.

There are no varieties, although a narrow-leaved form is available.

Site Sunny, protected
Soil Most, well-drained
Plant Spring
Harvest As required; or pick, dry, and store leaves.

Borage
Borago officinalis

Borage is one of the most decorative of all herbs, with brilliant blue flowers and hairy, oval leaves (in some soils, the flowers may be purplish or even clear pink). It is an annual but it will usually seed itself and come up somewhere: transplant the seedlings if they are in the wrong place. Under ideal conditions it may grow to about 1·2 m (4 ft) and be quite bushy, but more usually the height is between 450–750 mm (18–30 in). Such an attractive plant should really be grown where it may be seen; but, owing to its self-seeding, take care where you site it.

Sow in March to June. The seeds are large and may be sown individually, about 450 mm (18 in) apart. Water the soil lightly, press a seed in, cover with soil, and water again.

The soil should preferably be well draining; if it is very heavy, lighten it with sharp sand and peat, and compost if you have any to spare. The site should be sunny.

The flowers may be used when available to decorate drinks and salads. The leaves may be eaten raw for their cucumbery flavour, but their bristly hairs are not very appetising, so the leaves should be finely chopped. They may be blended into butter, yogurt, and cream or cottage cheese, or cooked as spinach.

Site Preferably sunny
Soil Well drained, not too heavy
Sow March–June
Harvest As required

Chervil
Anthriscus cerefolium

A fine-leaved, hardy, annual herb with rather carrot-like foliage but more spreading. The unusual flavour of the leaves, which is described by some as like aniseed, is excellent with egg dishes and soups, but as it is volatile the leaves should be added only towards the end of cooking.

It may be sown in March for summer use or late summer and autumn for winter harvesting. Sow as thinly as possible where the plants are to grow, cover with a sprinkling of soil, and water in. When the plants start growing away, thin as necessary to intervals of about 150 mm (6 in). Keep the soil weed-free. Once established, chervil should last for some years by self-sown seedlings. It is also easily raised and grown on in pots.

Site Open, or in pots
Soil Rich and fairly moist
Sow In spring for summer crops; in late summer and autumn for winter
Harvest Summer or winter, depending on sowing times

Chives and Chinese chives
Allium schoenoprasum and A. tuberosum

These excellent decorative perennials may easily be grown in borders, tubs, or pots. Most people are familiar with the hollow, round leaves of chives used in soups, salads, omelettes and other dishes. The less-common Chinese chives has flatter, solid leaves with a stronger flavour. The flowers of both are decorative; the rosy lilac common chives flowers appear in summer, just above the leaves, and the white flowers of Chinese chives grow in autumn on stiff stems above the arching leaves. Common chives plants usually grow about 200–250 mm (8–10 in) high, while the flower stems of Chinese chives may be up to 700 mm (28 in) high; the height of the latter must be allowed for if you are raising the plants in a decorative border. Common chives is also an excellent window-box plant, or it may be grown indoors in pots for earlier crops.

It is usual to buy clumps or the bulbous roots of chives, although they may also be raised from seed sown where they are to grow in March: seedlings do not transplant well. Plants are usually available in spring and autumn for planting up. Chives grow best in sunny sites with partial shade – but do not provide too much shade or the plants will get straggly and may die. The soil should be fairly rich and well-drained.

Clumps should be divided every few years, in the spring or autumn, and the divisions either replanted in new sites out of doors or (in the case of common chives) potted up for indoor use. Pots of the autumn divisions may be left outside until required, and then brought indoors to start fresh growth.

Harvest the leaves during the summer and autumn, but do not remove all the leaves from one plant or clump (for this reason it is advisable to grow several clumps). The flowers may also be eaten in bud and when just opening, and make a decorative addition to salads or soups. If seed is needed, leave a few heads to mature; but remember to remove

them or you might have a problem with self-sown seedlings.

Site Semi-shaded
Soil Most, well-drained
Sow or divide Sow in spring; divide clumps in spring or autumn
Harvest Summer and autumn

Coriander
Coriandrum sativum

Coriander is a herb or spice for curry lovers. The leaves provide a herb for curries; the seeds, which have a different flavour, are used to spice curries, pickles, and stews. The plants grow 500–600 mm (20–24 in) high.

Sow enough for about 10 plants in spring in the main plot, about 100 mm (4 in) apart. Thin to the strongest seedling if more than one germinates at each point. The seeds may also be sown in pots of bought compost; remember to keep them watered. Soil should be moderately rich and well-drained; if it lacks humus, add some compost a few weeks before sowing.

Harvest the leaves when the plants are nearly fully grown, but before flowering; by then they should have maximum flavour. They may be stored by quick freezing. Harvest the seeds when the seed capsules are yellow and ripe in autumn. Cut the whole plant off and hang it up in a dry, airy place. When fully dry the seeds may be shaken and rubbed out and stored in jars.

Site Sunny
Soil Most types, well-drained
Sow Spring
Harvest Leaves in summer before plants are fully grown; seeds when ripe in autumn

Dill
Anethum (Peucedanum) graveolens

Dill is an annual grown for its leaves and seeds: its young leaves are used in a similar manner to fennel's and in various sour dishes, and the seeds are rather similar to caraway; both leaves and seeds are used in pickles, especially for pickling cucumbers and

gherkins. The plants grow anything from 400–900 mm (16–36 in) high and will often self sow. The leaves are best preserved by quick freezing.

Sow in April to June; two or three plants will be sufficient for an average family's needs. Sow one or two seeds at each growing point, with about 300 mm (12 in) between each point; lightly cover with soil, and water in. Thin later to the strongest seedlings. The site should be sunny and protected from the wind. Most well-drained soils are suitable. Keep the soil weed-free.

Harvest the young leaves when the plants are beginning to get bushy. The seed should be harvested just before it is ripe, as it scatters easily. When the seed capsules are beginning to turn brown, cut the heads off and hang them in an airy, dry place.

Site Sunny, sheltered
Soil Most, well-drained
Sow April–June
Harvest Young leaves when required; seed capsules just before ripening

Fennel, Common and Florence
Foeniculum vulgare

Common and Florence fennel (also known as finnochio) are two forms of the same species. Although Florence fennel is better known as a vegetable – its swollen stem bases, resembling bulbous-ended celery, may be eaten raw or cooked – it is included here because its leaves, like those of common fennel, are used for flavouring sauces and pickles and with grilled fish. Common fennel is a decorative plant, available also in a golden-leaved form suitable for an ornamental part of the garden. It is a bushy perennial growing about 1·8 m (6 ft) high and seeds itself freely; the seeds are also used for flavouring. Florence fennel grows to about 600 mm (2 ft), but as it is dug up for use it gets no chance to seed itself and is best

The young flower buds of chives add colour to the flower border, as do the leaves of the variegated form of balm, on the right.

For flavouring, the leaves of Florence fennel (finnochio) make a useful substitute for those of the common form. The swollen stem bases of Florence fennel, seen here, are anise-flavoured and may be eaten raw or cooked; they can be blanched by earthing them up or covering them with a cardboard collar as they begin to swell.

planted in the kitchen garden. One or two plants of common fennel will be sufficient for most families; grow as many Florence fennel plants as you feel you might need – the flavour is rather aniseedy.

Fennel may be sown at most times of the year, but April is probably the most convenient time; in the common form growing points should be about 300 mm (12 in) apart. Common fennel may also be bought as a small potted herb. Sow Florence fennel in small blocks with the plants about 150–200 mm (6–8 in) apart.

A sunny, well-drained site is best for both types, and Florence fennel must be kept moist to swell the stem bases. Most soils in good condition are suitable; before sowing, sprinkle on a dusting of general fertiliser. Keep the soil weed-free.

Slugs and snails are especially fond of Florence fennel, and pellets should be sprinkled to prevent their attacks. Greenfly may infest the flower heads and can be dealt with by use of a suitable insecticide.

Common fennel is harvestable as soon as sufficient leaves have developed. To keep up a supply, cut a few shoots down to the base; new ones will quickly bush up. Florence fennel should be harvested when the stem bases are swollen; thereafter the leaves may be picked as required. Some people blanch the Florence fennel bases by placing a cardboard col-

lar around them for a while before harvesting; soil or peat can also be used for this purpose. Leaves of both forms may be preserved by deep freezing.

Varieties of fennel are seldom offered, although the golden form of common fennel is sometimes available. The Florence fennel variety 'Perfection' is recommended but is not often available.

Site Sunny
Soil Most, well-drained but moisture-retentive
Sow Spring
Harvest As required in summer and autumn

Garlic
Allium sativum

Regarded by many cooks as essential seasoning in a variety of dishes, garlic is fairly expensive to buy but easy to grow. A bulbous plant that takes up little room, it may be grown as an edging to other crops or to borders. When mature the bulbs are composed of a number of small, flattish bulbs or cloves; these are the pieces used in cooking and from which the crop is grown.

Plant the cloves 40–50 mm (1½–2 in) deep and about 100–125 mm (4–5 in) apart, and firm them in. The larger, outer cloves on the bulb are best. In particularly warm areas with sheltered gardens the cloves may be planted in the autumn; otherwise, plant in February to March. The soil should be enriched with compost some time before planting, and must be well-drained. The site should be sunny. Keep the soil weed-free and well watered in dry weather.

When the stems are about 150 mm (6 in) high, feed the plants with a high-nitrogen fertiliser. Then in early July, before the leaves start to turn yellow, apply a potash fertiliser.

Harvest in July to August after the leaves have yellowed. The whole plants should be lifted and hung in an airy place indoors to dry off.

Site Sunny
Soil Good, well-drained
Plant February–March
Harvest July–August

Horseradish
Armoracia rusticana

Horseradish is easy to grow, but high-quality roots – which are grated for making into a cream sauce used with roast meats and some fish – depend on good cultivation. Although the plant is a perennial it is wise to lift it every year to prevent too great a spread, which may become extremely difficult to get rid of. Large clusters of dock-like leaves about 600 mm (2 ft) long are formed, the first few being deeply divided. Flower stems may exceed 1·2 m (4 ft) but they rarely set seed.

The plot is prepared by digging holes about 600 mm (2 ft) deep and about 300 mm (1 ft) apart. Thoroughly mix compost with the removed soil before replacing it. Plant a piece of root (called a thong) 200–250 mm (8 –10 in) long vertically in each hole in February or March. The thongs need to be covered by about 100 mm (4 in) of soil. Firm them in and add water. The plants grow best on a light, well-drained soil, preferably in sun or partial shade; heavy soils should be lightened with peat and sharp sand.

Harvest from late summer onwards by lifting roots as required, and eventually clear the entire site. Surplus roots may be stored in the same way as carrots in a box of sand. They can be used later in the kitchen or for raising the next year's crop.

Site Most
Soil Well-draining, enriched
Plant February–March
Harvest Late summer to autumn

Hyssop
Hyssopus officinalis

Hyssop is a very attractive perennial, nearly evergreen herb bearing deep-blue flowers in summer and autumn. Grow it in a flower border to save space in the kitchen beds. It is easy to raise (although not absolutely hardy) and makes a bushy plant up to about 600 mm (2 ft) tall. Its bitter leaves are used in liqueurs, stews, stuffings, and soups in moderation, and the dried leaves also in pot-pourri. One or two plants will provide enough leaves for most families, but as it is not fully hardy it is wise to raise a

When in flower, hyssop enhances any border – although by then its leaves will be beginning to lose their flavour.

Common marjoram

Sweet marjoram

Marjoram 'Aureum'   Pot marjoram

Spearmint   French mint

Round-leaved mint

couple of extra ones every year – someone will almost certainly appreciate your surplus leaves – or the plants, spaced 250–300 mm (10–12 in) apart, may be used as a dwarf hedge. Although blue-flowered hyssop is commonest, pink- and white-flowered forms are occasionally obtainable.

Sow two or three seeds under the protection of a cloche or cold frame in March in 75 mm (3 in) pots of potting compost, or unprotected where the plant is to grow in April to May. Thin the seedlings to the strongest plant in each pot or position. Plants raised under protection or bought should be planted out in the autumn. A sunny, well-drained site is best; lighten heavy soils with sharp sand and peat. After the plants flower, trim off the dead flower heads (unless you wish to save seed), and in March prune the plants to a height of about 75 mm (3 in) to encourage bushy growth.

Harvest the leaves as required. As with most herbs, the flavour of the leaves is best before flowering. Use young leaves for drying.

Site Sunny
Soil Light, well-drained
Sow March if protected; April–May if unprotected
Harvest As required

Marjoram
Origanum species

Of the three main species of marjoram used for flavouring only one, *Origanum majorana*, the sweet or knotted marjoram, is widely available as seed. The other two, *O. vulgare*, common or wild marjoram (oregano), and *O. onites*, pot marjoram, are hardier perennials and are often available as pot-grown herbs from nurseries and garden centres. They all have distinct aromas, the sweet marjoram being particularly fragrant, and pot marjoram less so. In a small garden it is probably best to grow only sweet and common marjoram – the first for its richness, the second for its hardiness. Common marjoram has a golden-leaved form, *O. vulgare* 'Aureum', which makes a brilliant yellow-green carpet

in early spring and late autumn (but more of a hummock in summer) and is quite suitable for a decorative border or for a rock garden. In flower it grows to about 600 mm (2 ft) in height. Sweet marjoram grows to about 200 mm (8 in). Common marjoram is not as strong-flavoured as the oregano grown in Italy, but it is used in the same way for many dishes, including pizza, pork dishes, poultry, and game. Sweet marjoram should be added to dishes just before cooking ceases, as its flavour is volatile. Both herbs may be dried. One or two plants of each should be sufficient for most families.

Sweet marjoram is grown from seed sown in late February or March. It may be sown into 75 mm (3 in) pots of potting compost. Two seeds in the centre of each pot should be just covered with the compost and watered in; thin later to the stronger seedling. The pots can be placed outdoors under cloches or in a frame. Harden the plants off and in May either plant out where they are to grow, about 200 mm (8 in) apart, or pot on into 125 mm (5 in) pots to grow on.

Alternatively, you can sow direct into the ground where they are to grow in May. Common marjoram should be planted where it is to grow in spring or autumn or raised from seed as for sweet marjoram. Once established it may be increased by dividing the clumps and replanting them where required in early spring. If the plants are grown in the soil, a sunny, well-drained site, preferably on the limy side, is best for both species. While common marjoram may more or less be left to fend for itself except in extremes of weather, sweet marjoram should be kept growing well and kept moist. When several leaves have formed, pinch out the growing tips to make the plants more bushy.

Harvest the leaves when young and fresh as required.

Site Sunny, sheltered
Soil Well drained, alkaline; add lime if necessary
Sow Early spring under protection; late spring in the open
Harvest As required when the plants are large enough; common and sweet types can be dried and stored

Mint
Mentha species

Most mints are unsuitable for growing in open ground in small gardens because they tend to spread rapidly. Different mints are used for different purposes such as flavouring for confectionery, liqueurs, and so on, but French mint, *Mentha* × *villosa alopecuroides*, and round-leaved mint, *M. suaveolens*, will fulfil most culinary requirements. Many people are also fond of the flavour of the coarser spearmint, *M. spicata*.

In the smaller garden or for those with paved areas, these mints must be confined and will do well in suitably sized pots; all are decorative. French mint, also known as Bowles or woolly mint, grows up to 1·2 m (4 ft) in height, as does round-leaved; spearmint is rather smaller. Round-leaved mint also has a variegated-leaved form 'Variegata', known as pineapple mint, which is even more decorative.

Mint is usually raised from pieces of rooted runners that are cut off and replanted or are sold ready-planted in small pots. Whichever you use, pot them up into 200–250 mm (8–10 in) pots – the pieces of root preferably in February or March, and pot-grown plants at any time. The pots should contain potting compost enriched with well-rotted garden compost. Place the rooted piece or plant in the centre, firm it in, and water. A half-shaded or more sunny position is suitable. Keep the compost moist at all times. To ensure supplies of fresh leaves, cut down any flower stems that develop; the flavour deteriorates after flowering. Add a top dressing of garden compost in late winter.

Replace the plants every two or three years by cutting off a fresh piece of rooted runner and replanting it in a fresh pot.

Pests are rarely a trouble, but the plants may be attacked by leaf rust. Any plants so affected should be burnt.

Harvest the leaves as required.

Site Half-shaded to sunny
Soil Rich
Plant Early spring
Harvest As required

Parsley
Petroselinum crispum

An essential herb, used widely in fish sauces and in salads, parsley is easily grown although it is sometimes slow to germinate from seed. Re-sow it annually if self-sown seedlings do not appear. Most seedsmen list several varieties, but there is little to choose between them from the culinary point of view.

Sow a few seeds in spring at a depth of 12–20 mm (½–¾ in) where the plants are to grow, and thin out later to space the plants 200–250 mm (8–10 in) apart. The soil should be enriched with compost in autumn or

Parsley is sometimes slow to germinate, but if you allow two or three flower heads to set seed, self-sown plants should appear. Failing that, sow seeds in spring.

winter and allowed to settle. It needs to be free-draining, and the plants should be watered in dry weather. Parsley prefers a sunny or lightly shaded site.

Harvest as required when the plants are large enough. Cutting back the plants in autumn and covering them with cloches may provide leaves for winter use.

Site Sunny
Soil Good, rich
Sow Spring
Harvest As required

Rosemary
Rosmarinus officinalis

Rosemary is an excellent evergreen shrub to decorate a border or patio; for the latter it may be grown in large pots or tubs. Although it is not completely hardy it is well worth growing, especially in small, sheltered gardens in towns, where it will benefit from the extra warmth. Besides its well known use with lamb, it may also be used when grilling poultry, fish, and other meats, and in stews; if added to a barbecue fire, it will scent the air.

Rosemary is usually raised from pot-grown plants obtainable from nurseries and garden centres. While one or two well-established bushes will be enough for most families, always keep a reserve of a few cuttings growing on in case of disaster over winter. Plant in a sheltered, sunny site in well-drained soil in

The 'Purpurascens' cultivar of sage makes an attractive addition to a flower border.

autumn or spring.

Propagate by taking cuttings in late summer or early autumn. Cleanly cut off two or three 50–75 mm (2–3 in) ends of stems, trim off the lower leaves, and dip the cut ends in rooting powder. Now insert the cuttings, to the level of the lowest remaining leaves, around the edge of a small pot filled with cutting compost. Firm the stems gently and water the cuttings in. Keep the cuttings protected throughout the winter in a frame, under cloches, or inside a shed beside a window. Keep the compost just moist. In the spring, gradually harden the cuttings off and plant them out where they are to grow or in larger pots filled with potting compost.

Harvest the leafy twigs as required by cutting them off with secateurs or a sharp knife. The leaves dry well for storing in an airtight container.

Recommended varieties The following have little to differentiate them from the culinary point of view, but vary in habit or flower colour. *R.*

officinalis, the type plant, grows to about 2 m (6½ ft), but usually less, and bears lilac-blue flowers; 'Albus' is white flowered; 'Fastigiatus' ('Miss Jessup's Variety', 'Jessup's Upright'), grows compactly upright; 'Roseus' bears lilac-pink flowers; 'Severn Sea' is a dwarf with gracefully arched branches and brighter-blue flowers

Site Sunny, sheltered
Soil Well-drained
Plant Spring or autumn
Harvest All the year as required

Sage
Salvia officinalis

Sage is another ornamental shrubby herb suitable for growing in a border or large container to relieve pressure on space in the small kitchen garden. It is used in stuffings and to flavour pork, game, poultry (but not chicken), and some fish dishes. An evergreen, it may lose its leaves or even die in very bad winters. It grows to about 600 mm (2 ft) in height. There are several forms with coloured leaves, which increase the decorative effect, but for flavour the broadleaved form of the common sage is considered superior. Plants raised from seed may be well-flavoured, but to get the best leaves you should buy pot-grown plants of the type required and increase them by cuttings, as for rosemary.

A sunny well drained site is preferable with soil on the alkaline (limy or chalky) side. Sage is a rather straggly plant and should be kept trimmed every year. Branches which touch the ground often take root; these may be cut off and replanted.

Harvest the leaves as required.

Recommended varieties *S. officinalis*, the type plant, broad-leaved with grey-green leaves, is the best culinary form; 'Icterina' bears yellow-splashed leaves; 'Purpurascens' has purplish leaves and stems; 'Tricolor' has leaves splashed pink, white, and purple

Site Sunny
Soil Well-drained, alkaline
Plant Spring or autumn
Harvest All the year

Savory
Satureia species

Two savories are commonly grown –
the annual summer-harvested species, *Satureia hortensis*, and the almost
evergreen, shrubby, perennial winter
species, *S. montana*. Summer savory
has a milder, sweeter flavour but
both herbs are used in the same way
for flavouring soups, stews, pork,
salads, and other dishes. Winter savory makes a fine dwarf edging plant
for a border. Both are easy to grow,
summer savory from seed and winter
savory from pot-grown plants. Both
attain a height of up to 300 mm
(12 in), but winter savory has a more
spreading, bushy habit than the summer species.

Sow summer savory in April,
either in a garden plot where it is to
grow or in pots. Sow two or three
seeds at each growing point and thin
them later to leave the strongest. In
the plot the plants should be spaced
150 mm (6 in) apart. Lightly cover the
seeds with soil and water them in but
do not oversoak.

*Winter savory, unlike the summer form, is an
almost evergreen perennial, useful when few
other fresh herbs are available.*

Plant out pot-grown winter savory
in April or September, spacing the
plants 250 mm (10 in) apart. Both species prefer a good, fairly light, well-
drained soil in a sunny site. Start
pot-grown summer savory in 90 mm
(3½ in) pots of John Innes potting
compost No 1 and pot on later to
125 mm (5 in) pots using John Innes
No 2 or 3. Keep the compost moist at
all times.

French tarragon is an especially good herb for flavouring bland dishes. It can readily be grown in pots or tubs.

Harvest the sprigs when required. Winter savory can be harvested almost the whole year, and summer savory from June onwards. Winter savory plants should be cut back in early spring to encourage fresh young growth to develop.

Site Sunny
Soil Good, light, well-drained
Sow Summer savory in March
Plant Summer savory in April; winter savory in April or September
Harvest Summer savory from June to late autumn; winter savory most of the year

Sorrel
Rumex acetosa and *R. scutatus*

These excellent perennials are easy to grow. They have very similar flavours and may be used in a wide variety of dishes, including soups, omelettes, and pork, and in sour sauces; they may also be used fresh in salads. Common or garden sorrel, *R. acetosa*, is unfortunately rarely available from seedsmen, who usually stock the more acid *R. scutatus* under the name French or Large sorrel. The plants will grow to a height of 600 mm (2 ft) or more if allowed to flower, but regular cutting should prevent this.

Sow a few seeds in April where the plants are to grow. The seeds are large and should be sown 12–20 mm (½–¾ in) deep, with two or three at each growing point, and thinned later. The plants should be 300 mm (12 in) apart. Sorrel will grow on most soils but needs to be kept moist. To get the best leaves, grow the plants in a semi-shaded site; in constant direct sunlight the leaves may be less fleshy. To encourage leaf growth the flowering shoots should be pinched out as they appear.

Harvest the leaves as required from summer onwards.

Site Semi-shaded
Soil Most types; keep moist
Sow April
Harvest Summer onwards

Tarragon
Artemisia dracunculus sativa

Tarragon, a perennial plant, is available in two forms – Russian, *A. dracunculus inodora*, and French, *A. dracunculus sativa*. Buy only the French variety: Russian tarragon is greatly inferior in quality and, unlike French, will readily set seed. French tarragon is a superb herb, so good that even the most pallid frozen fowls become transformed when flavoured with its leaves. It is also added to fish dishes, casseroles, and salads and used for flavouring wine vinegar. It is not absolutely hardy, so it is sensible to buy young plants in the spring to avoid losses over the first winter. The plants are usually sold in 50 or 75 mm (2 or 3 in) pots. Although they can be planted out in the garden, they will thrive in pots and so save space in your kitchen plot. Immediately after purchase, pot on the plants into 125 or 150 mm (5 or 6 in) pots with John Innes No 2 or 3. Later in the season pot on again, into 180 or 230 mm (7 or 9 in) pots, using similar compost. Keep the compost moist and feed the plants regularly with a diluted liquid fertiliser. As you pot up into the larger pots, a small portion of each plant should be carefully prised away (make sure it has roots as well as a stem portion) and planted in a small pot with JI No 2. These divisions should be taken in the summer so that the young plants can gain strength before the winter. Keep the divisions in a more sheltered spot than the main plants in case of loss. As the plants age they tend to deteriorate and the new plants you have started should then be used to replace them, with the same procedure of potting on being carried out. Tarragon favours a warm, sunny site, preferably against a south-west-facing wall; it will reach a height of 600–900 mm (2–3 ft).

Harvest the young stems with leaves as required. If you are using the leaves to flavour wine vinegar, make sure they are thoroughly dry.

Site Sunny, sheltered
Soil JI No 2 or 3 compost; or most well-drained soils
Plant Spring
Harvest As required

Thyme
Thymus species and varieties

There is a large number of evergreen thyme varieties available. Most are grown for ornamental purposes but, as with the culinary varieties of *T. vulgaris*, the aromatic flavour in their leaves varies in intensity; some are very good indeed, and others less so. If you are already growing some variety of ornamental thyme, try it for flavour! The herb is excellent for pork dishes, casseroles, and in stuffings for savory dishes. Thymes vary greatly in leaf and form. The leaves may be anything from small and spear-shaped to round, and from light yellow-green in colour to dark bluish green or green with yellow or white variegations. Some varieties of *T. citriodorus* have a flavour like lemon, orange, or other herbs. They vary in form from mats to bushy plants up to 300 mm (12 in) high.

As with many other herbs, thyme varieties are best raised from bought pot-grown plants. These should be potted on as for tarragon, but using *smaller* pots at each stage; alternatively, they may be planted out. They grow in most well-drained soils, preferably slightly alkaline. The prostrate varieties root as they form mats and can be propagated by detaching small rooted pieces and planting them elsewhere or potting them up. The upright-growing varieties can also be increased by division or by using the self-sown seedlings. Most varieties will also root readily from cuttings, about 30 mm (1¼ in) long, treated as for rosemary. The bushy upright varieties should be trimmed after flowering.

Harvest the leaves as required.

Varieties
COMMON, GARDEN, OR FRENCH THYME Bushy
LEMON THYME Several forms, including 'Silver Queen' with silver variegated leaves; bushy to prostrate
CARAWAY THYME Prostrate
GOLDEN THYME Mat-forming, mild-flavoured

Site Sunny, sheltered
Soil Well-drained
Plant Immediately after purchase
Harvest As required

Index

Acknowledgements

The publishers wish to thank the following organizations and individuals for their kind permission to reproduce the photographs in this book:
A–Z Botanical Collection Ltd 12–13; Bernard Alfieri 14, 37, 44; Pat Brindley 53 inset; Brian Furner 33, 47, above, 48, 51, 57, 60 inset, 64, 68, 73, 75, 76; Harry Smith Horticultural Photographic Collection 24, 27, 29, 30 inset, 35, 36, 38, 47 below, 55, 60–61, 65, 71, 72, 77; Sutton's Seeds (Torquay) Ltd 60; Michael Warren 1, 9, 20, 30–31, 41, 45, 52–53, 59; Tom Wellsted 78
Special Photography: Peter Rauter 2–3, 4–5, 6–7, 10–11, 16–17, 22–23, 66–67; Jacket Photography: Ron Sutherland
Drawings: Liz Pepperell 32, 34, 50, 61 (inset), 74; Ed Stewart 19, 25, 40, 56, 61; Eric Thomas 42–3; Tudor Art Studios 15, 21, 42 (top), 46
The publishers are grateful for the help of Charles and D.W. Butters, Garden Cottage, Stow Randolph Hall, Norfolk.